DO THEY SPEAK ENGLISH DOWN THERE?

From duct tape to #8 wire . . .
creating a life in New Zealand.

This book is dedicated to my husband, an ode to his courage in embracing a sweeping lifestyle change, and to our two children who clinched this adventure with enthusiasm and positivity.

Special thanks to fellow Wellington writer, Blair Polly, for his technical expertise, professional support and patience; without whom this story would still be waiting to be told.

And special thanks to my dear friend, Linda Grace, for unwittingly suggesting the title.

DO THEY SPEAK ENGLISH DOWN THERE?

From duct tape to #8 wire . . .
creating a life in New Zealand.

SUSAN C. TUNNEY

Wainui

Press

Author's note:
While this story is based on my personal experiences, the
names and people in the story are purely fictional and
any resemblance to any living person is unintentional and
coincidental.

ISBN: 9781729224403
eISBN: 9781642370997

 **Wainui**
Press
Printed in the United States of America

Table of Contents

How It All Came About

THE COURSE OF MY LIFE was about to change after a headline in the Sunday *San Diego Union-Tribune* screamed: **Now is the Time to Visit New Zealand**. Ahhh, New Zealand: two words synonymous with beauty/ nature, outdoors/rugby and definitely not/Australia! The strong American dollar along with several breathtaking photographs of the unspoiled landscapes of *Lord of the Rings* fame fired my interest. Though, to be honest, I was the only one in our family who had not seen the film and still haven't to this day.

Included in the article were a few suggested itineraries, but the one that appealed to me most was the option of a motorhome rental. This would give us the freedom to explore the much-touted natural scenic wonders at our own pace and not have to worry about sourcing accommodation with its check-in and check-out restrictions. And it included a free stopover in Tahiti. I've been told opportunity frequently brings about change and, clearly, this was an opportunity not to be missed.

So, the hastily made vow I had made after 9/11 not to travel outside California was quickly broken. In less than two months after the World Trade Center buildings fell, here I was booking a flight to Auckland with a four-night detour through Tahiti. Back then, we were an angry nation, paralyzed with fear; our smug sense of security abruptly shattered by the all-too-evident anti-American sentiments in the world. Daily the media pounded us with color-coded alerts for potential attacks against the homeland that thrust us into a chronic state of hyper-vigilance. But New Zealand, geographically tucked as it is at the bottom of the world with its people mostly minding their own business, somehow felt safe enough for our family to venture out of the country for the first time since the terrorist attacks.

And what a great time to travel it proved to be, in that Los Angeles International airport was like a ghost town with no crowds, no long queues, no hassles! Not so today, as even with 9/11 a more distant memory, security precautions remain heightened and LAX has become one of the least-desirable airports through which to transit in the USA, if not the world.

As the trip had to be booked around the school holidays, I was unsure about the best time weather-wise to visit New Zealand. Our travel agent referred me to the toll-free number of the motorhome rental agency in New Zealand, but by some weird fluke, I found myself speaking to a young girl in an automotive parts store somewhere in south Auckland. Well, figuring she was native and therefore knowledgeable, I engaged her a few minutes and asked her opinion. Without hesitation, she advised me, as she would have done friends, to come visit during the latter part of August, rather than May, which she insisted was a rather nasty month. August, she told me thoughtfully with an English-sounding accent, was a time of "rebirth," with spring blossoms appearing on trees and baby lambs bleating in fields all over the country. Ahhh . . . it all sounded just so idyllic, so pristine. So very *Hobbit-ish.*

And thus, it was a few months later, after languishing at an overpriced resort in Moorea for four nights, we packed our swimsuits and sandals at the bottom of the suitcases, donned turtleneck sweaters, fleece jackets and jeans, and boarded the plane, prepared for winter in Auckland.

When the clouds parted seven hours or so after leaving Tahiti and the plane touched the ground in New Zealand, I was reminded of Bill Bryson's comments in his book *In a Sunburned Country* upon visiting Australia for the first time. It dawned on me that all I really knew about the country was indeed very little.

In fact, it amounted to only a few comments from my geography teacher in Northern Ireland, namely that it had an economy based primarily on agriculture and sheep farming. Okay? I didn't know if it was completely independent from Great Britain. How it governed its people, or who, exactly, was the president, assuming there was a president. Or did they elect a prime minister? After all, mostly everyone in the world knows who the president of the United States is at any given time.

I didn't know any New Zealanders personally and remembered only ever having met one on a bus in Fiji many years before while traveling the South Pacific with my husband before our marriage. Americans were more familiar with the Australian stereotype of the brash, rugged adventurer such as the late Steve Irwin, and "Come and say g'day" Paul Hogan with his invitation: "I'll slip an extra shrimp on the barbie for you" fame.

But I had seen the Jane Campion film *The Piano* and as a result expected the country to be a rather quaint Southern Hemisphere interpretation of England, with half-clothed tattooed natives popping up randomly from the bush.

It was the cool sharpness of the air that impressed me immediately when I breathed deeply the brisk outdoors upon clearing customs in Auckland which was a breeze compared to the U.S. New Zealand was more concerned about any food items or honey we may be bringing into their protected environment rather than a potential terrorist threat. Exiting the international terminal, I was immediately taken with the air filling my lungs; so invigorating, so crisp and in a word: fresh.

The sun felt intense and very warm on my face when the few clouds parted enough to let it peek through and the temperature was mild as an early autumn day rather than having the bite of the middle of winter. As we made our way to the motorhome rental agency across the parking lot in front of the airport, I noted the contours of the surrounding landscape and the lush, softly rolling green hills. Everything appeared very sharp in the pollution-free air. The surrounding fields were intensely green in the bright sunlight, which now flashed its rays in full glory from a cloudless deep blue sky, unencumbered by an intact ozone layer.

After a brief orientation to the operation of the motorhome, which we quickly christened The Beast, and a quick shop at a nearby grocery store to load up on provisions, we were on our way. Secure with maps in hand, we began to make our way towards a campground somewhere north of Auckland. Why we were heading north was a bit of a mystery to me, as we had made our plans quite clear to the young man at the agency that getting to the South Island over the next few days was a top priority.

With The Beast now packed to capacity, we hummed along excitedly on the main artery out of Auckland, driving past rows and rows of moored yachts bobbing contentedly in the harbor, and all seemed well with the world. Soon we would be settling in at a lovely park-like campground for the night and cooking our first meal in the land of the Lord of the Rings, Middle Earth.

Then we came to a complete stop.

"Hey! What's this?" I asked. "And where are all these cars coming from? I thought there were no people in New Zealand? Honestly, this is as bad as L.A., for God's sake."

A half-hour later, we had barely moved a mile. "This is ridiculous! Do you think there's been an accident or something?" I asked, looking back out the window at the long line of bumper-to-bumper cars behind us.

The lanes seemed to grow narrower as we crept towards the Auckland Harbor Bridge. It was well after 5 p.m. now; it being August and wintertime in the southern hemisphere, dusk was quickly upon us. Suddenly, blue skies gave way to dense black cloud cover that soon belted out thick pellets of torrential rain against our windshield, greatly compromising what little visibility we had achieved as we crawled onto the bridge. The windshield wipers were whipping furiously across the huge expanse of glass; my husband sat and struggled to stay focused on the present challenges, i.e. staying in his lane, and on the left-hand side of the road.

"Oh damn! Where are the lights in this thing?" Paul called with a sense of urgency as he fiddled around the steering wheel. "Alex, keep a look out on my left, please," he asked our teenage son, the navigator.

"God! These roads are narrow. Am I in the right lane . . . I mean the *correct* lane here? Jesus, fella! Did you see that guy? He completely cut me off," Paul yelled, shaking his head in disbelief.

Well, so much for the relaxed, laid-back Kiwi persona touted in every tourist brochure I had read back home. Despite Paul's patient and polite efforts, no one was making room for The Beast to move over a lane. The rumpled Tahitian-themed shirt Paul was wearing now looked a bit comical and belied his frustration after he missed the first exit, then the second one.

Suddenly, he sat up straight and determined he would not stay a moment longer on this crowded motorway. "Well, like it or not, buddy, here I come," he said to no one directly as he veered The Beast over to the next lane towards the exit while horns blasted in irritation from all sides.

"What is the deal here? Good Lord! Are you friggin' sure we're in New Zealand?" I called from the back seat, unraveling quickly at this stage.

The familiar knot between my shoulders slowly snaked its way up my back, winding towards my neck. All the hard-earned Polynesian relaxation achieved over the last four days vanished within just two hours of our arrival to New Zealand. Ah, but how was I to know the fun was only beginning?

For well over an hour, we drove around in circles, in heavy drizzle, on poorly lit roads, with no signage anywhere, searching for the campground highlighted on our map. To this day, I still have no idea where we actually were, except that it was in the middle of Auckland suburbia, a bit north of Devonport. Who in their right mind would place a campground in the middle of a town? And what an idiot that fellow was at the rental agency to direct us overseas folk to drive north over the Harbor Bridge, in a huge motorhome, in the middle of Friday afternoon rush-hour traffic in Auckland. Hmmm.

While Paul connected the vehicle to the necessary services in our assigned space at the campground, I poured a healthy shot of duty-free vodka into some fruit juice and sat outside at a picnic table. I had barely taken my first sip when a male voice called from behind me. I turned around to see a young man walking towards my table, my space. Really! All I wanted was to be left alone for five minutes or so until the alcohol took effect, then I'd be right. But no, now I was forced to be polite and make small conversation.

"Hi there. So, you've just arrived? How are ya finding the place?" he asked, pushing his hands deep into his jean pockets.

"Well, to be perfectly honest with you, we've just had the ride from hell here from the city. I mean to say I was led to believe there were more sheep than people in New Zealand, for goodness sake. So far, I've seen way too many people and no sheep. I'm telling you, that drive from the airport was just as bad as any commute in Southern California. I could not believe how rude the drivers were. No one would let us over a lane to exit. Talk about road rage . . . you know, honestly, you could get shot for that kind of stuff in L.A.."

Our fellow camper laughed and held out his hand and introduced himself as Tim, a visitor from England. He was winding down a six-month trip visiting his brother down in Queenstown and touring the South Island.

"Ah, just wait till you get out of Auckland area," he promised, "and to the South Island especially. Absolutely gorgeous. I hope you make it down there as you'll see New Zealand at its best. There is absolutely no one on the roads for miles and miles! And you will see your fields and fields of sheep. Promise. Just glorious, unspoiled, uncluttered scenery. Truly."

I smiled. "Now, that's what I'm talking about. Sounds fantastic. I certainly didn't come here to complain about traffic, that's for sure. We're from San Diego, by the way. On a two-week family holiday, which I really hope doesn't become a two-week family nightmare given the rather stressful start to this trip. Actually, our plan is to spend as much time as possible in the South Island, so why in God's name that clown in the rental agency by the airport directed us here for the night, I'll never know."

"Hmm. You're not giving yourselves much time at all, eh? Two weeks?" He said, shaking his head. "And you want to cover most of this country? But, then again, you Americans tend to whip around at an extraordinary pace."

"Are you still on about that drive here?" Paul smiled as he joined my side and introductions were made all round. Drinks were soon poured as we listened keenly to our camp mate, who shared insider information and recent travel experiences in New Zealand. Soon an hour or so had quickly passed and the kids were obviously getting a bit restless, hinting at wanting something to eat, when our fellow camper kindly suggested we might try the Pizza Hut near the entrance to the campgrounds.

Pizza Hut! What? You've got to be kidding! No way did I travel halfway around the globe to eat Pizza Hut in New Zealand, when I don't even eat it at home. Please! But the kids were hungry and pizza always works for a quick tasty fix in a pinch. Feeling less harried after my second drink, I decided I could indeed be sweet and acquiesce in their wishes. As we were getting ready to walk down the long, pebbled stone entryway, our friend hoped we would sleep well despite the rental units around us quickly filling up with young males.

"I hear a rugby club has booked all the rooms for the night," he informed us with some hesitation.

It would be a few hours later until the true implications of this statement became appallingly apparent.

"Swing low, sweet chariot . . . coming for to carry me home. Swi- ing lowww . . . ."

I don't know how long I had actually been asleep when I was awakened to boisterous cheering and pitchy singing outside our motorhome. As time wore on, it grew louder, more constant and terribly annoying. I peeked through the curtains and noticed that all the surrounding units were brightly lit, filled with men in striped jerseys laughing, slapping one another's backs, then breaking into yet another song:

"Why was he born so beautiful, why was he born at all . . . ?"

God help me. I looked at my watch and it was a bit after two a.m. By the looks of things, one would think it were only ten at night, as these fellows had no apparent plans to quit anytime soon. So, I lay awake, staring at the ceiling, serenaded by a bunch of drunken rugby players and the low-pitched drone of my husband's snoring.

Welcome to New Zealand . . . traffic jams, road rage, Pizza Hut and rowdy rugby parties.

But . . . where were the sheep?

An American Transplant

I T'S ALWAYS THE SAME REACTION when I begin to speak: the double take, the heightened attention. The curiosity. My accent is different. I am not a native New Zealander or Kiwi as they say here. Then the inevitable interrogation begins . . . "So, what brings you all the way from San Diego to Wairarapa?"

After living here since 2004, I can now have some fun with this question. "Oh, isn't it obvious?" I answer quite seriously. Well, obviously it is not. I mean to say, if someone from Wairarapa were to move to San Diego, the question might well begin with How, as in How the hell did you manage that stroke of luck, instead of *Why?* The why would be a given.

Sometimes there is a degree of circumspection in the questioning. "So, are you . . . Canadian?" This carefully posed P.C. question is intended to prevent a possible tirade from a would-be Canadian mistaken for American.

When I moved here, anti-American sentiment was running high in New Zealand with the Bush administration raging its war in Iraq and George W. Bush up again for re-election. Back then, though totally against my true nature, I was inclined to answer that question almost with a quiet apology. "No," I'd hesitate, "I'm . . . American." And then, I'd quickly add, "Irish-American," which was often received with immediate derision.

"What do you mean, Irish-American? You were born in America, correct? Then you're bloody well American, aren't you, mate?"

Plain and simple. Never mind that I'm a first-generation American born to Irish immigrants, who lived and was educated in northern Ireland during my teens. No, this didn't matter. I was judged purely on my American accent.

Today, though, I can answer this question with a bit more confidence as a New Zealand citizen when asked if I'm Canadian. I usually pause a moment in affected horror and say, "Canadian? Heavens, no. Who'd want to be a bloody Canadian? Actually, I'm American-born. Heaven forbid someone might mistake me for an Australian, eh?"

Discussion over.

Well, it has taken a few years living in New Zealand to get some goals realized, those listed as follows though in no particular order of importance:

- securing New Zealand citizenship,
- building a new house on eight acres of otherwise useless farming land with incredible views and surrounded by many happy sheep and dairy cattle,
- establishing a vegetable garden,
- celebrating our son graduating from Auckland Medical School and our daughter from Victoria University with a degree in business,
- both children still speaking to me regularly and professing love after all the vicissitudes of teenage years,
- my husband getting New Zealand medical registration and now practicing as a rural general surgeon and STILL my husband, and
- running a successful business from my house called Let's Do Lunch, a hands-on cooking class.

It's all-good, as they say here . . . BUT it hasn't been ALL-easy.

Today, I sit high on a hill in our custom-built house, living my days in the Land of the Long White Cloud, the name given to New Zealand by the native Māori and now the place I call home. In the end, I had to build a house to get exactly the purpose-built kitchen I had envisaged to lead cooking classes, not to mention we wanted double-glazing and maximum insulation to ensure a warm house. It had been a long-standing dream of Paul's to build his own house, and one that he had been priced out of in San Diego. Most houses here we found to be very cold and damp, with warmth being achieved only by "rugging-up" with several layers of clothing, burning wood and turning on the electric blanket before going to bed. I'm sorry, but this simply would not do, or contribute to a healthy indoor environment in winter at latitude forty-two below. It's hardly surprising therefore that New Zealand has one of the highest rates of asthma in the world. This is the South Pacific all right, but even though it's the North Island, it feels more like the Sweden of the South Pacific at times.

I awaken to a constantly changing canvas of nature, a view many in the world might only dare to dream about: empty, rolling, velvety green hills to the north and south of me, and dotted with sheep, lots of sheep! And thankfully, none of them mine to shepherd. I remember reading once that when the first English settlers were arriving en masse, the abundant numbers of sheep grazing in the hills were mistaken for boulders. Hills dotted with creamy-colored boulders everywhere.

From my windows, I can see cattle grazing below to the west in a well-tended, verdant and very productive dairy farm, bisected by a meandering river over a rocky bed which has its source somewhere in the wavy rows of the Tararua Mountains in the distance which frame this valley. This is New Zealand *Big Sky* country. Behind this lower North Island range, the sun sets many evenings as a flaming torch, spreading hues of orange, yellow and crimson across the expansive sky around our house as it bids the day farewell in air that is unpolluted and smog free. It's as if I had a huge digital screen in front of me, flashing new and varied pictures all throughout the day.

On days when there is dense cloud cover, I never see the mountains at all. But I always awaken to bird song or the loud squawking of black and white magpies. In summer when rainfall is scarce, the river is often running only a trickle, but can quickly and dramatically rise after a rainfall, flooding, and will completely cover much of the rocky riverbed. In winter, as it is now, the mountains are thickly snow-capped, reaching up to the blue sky in the distance, but this frosty scene can disappear with some sunshine by late afternoon. My husband tells me our water storage tanks are overflowing with all the recent rain, so I now take nightly baths without guilt. On early winter mornings, I can see across the valley to the town below in the distance, which is often enveloped in a layer of smoke from all the house fires lit during the evening for heat. And I happily reside above it all, nearer to the fast-moving clouds above me.

A feisty nor'wester is whistling now in all directions around my house, rocking the Adirondack chair in front of my office to and fro and bowing all vegetation in its wake, including my recently bloomed daffodils, to a humble 45-degree angle. The vernal equinox is a week away, and it's not unusual to have gusty gales this time of the year. Spring is just making itself felt. Rebirth. Baby lambs are bleating everywhere, seeking refuge under their mother's tummies, their tales wagging contentedly back and forth as they nurse with fierce determination.

A few years ago at this time of year, famous actors such as Orlando Bloom, the wizard Gandalf (Sir Ian McKellan), and Bilbo Baggins himself (Martin Freeman) were seen roaming the streets in Wellington in town to film *The Hobbit*. I really am living in Hobbitville! Or so the New Zealand tourism board tries hard to promote ad nauseam from the moment one boards a flight on Air New Zealand. Wellington now calls itself the Middle of Middle Earth . . . enough already! I get it. Trust me, there is way more to New Zealand than *Lord of the Rings* movie sets and characters.

I know I'm not in San Diego any longer when I wake sometimes to find a neighbor's sheep chomping away on cabbages in my vegetable garden in the courtyard off the kitchen, or look out the window and find myself face to face with a cow that has figured out how to go under the neighbor's electric wire fence to feast on my costly designer-grass border in the front of the house. While all my friends in California are talking about their sunny beach days in July, or taking their boats over to Catalina Island for long summer weekends with outdoor concerts and fireworks, I am bundling up and trying to find dry firewood in my shed to start the fire for the evening and wondering if it is ever going to stop raining. But, after all, July is middle of winter down here at the bottom of the world. Everything feels upside-down. What am I doing here . . . was I nuts to leave San Diego? I sometime still have doubts, but these have become less and less over the years.

Often I joke that the best thing about living in our town, Wairarapa, is that there is a train that leaves it several times a day to Wellington, the capital city, and I am often on it. The journey itself traverses some stunning topography. I can be there in a breezy hour and a half and catch a foreign film, eat some fantastic dim-sum, watch award-winning theatre, ballet or opera then spend the night in our modest one-bedroom apartment which overlooks the harbor, an entirely different scene. Wellington, with its vibrant urban energy, never fails to deliver and packs a huge punch for its size. Often, it is playfully referred to as *Wellywood* as it is the heart of the New Zealand film industry and, indeed, Hollywood stars can be spotted walking nonchalantly around the streets with a noticeable lack of paparazzi. But much to my dismay, the televised Academy Award celebrations hold minimal interest for folk.

Recently I was told that Brad Pitt was spotted in a local vineyard here in Wairarapa, quietly sipping a glass of wine with Sir Peter Jackson, who has built an impressive, secluded "country estate" in the western foothills. When people from around the country ask me how the hell did I end up in Wairarapa, I now joke that if the area is good enough for film directors such as Sir

Peter Jackson and recent new Canadian transplant named James Cameron, well then it's good enough for me, too.

But back to Wellington. The city is built around a horseshoe-shaped harbor and is relatively safe as far as big cities go, with no real pockets of crime-ridden "bad" areas and it's very easy to get around without a car. Once my daughter was bemoaning the fact that Wellington was too small and that she was, in fact, "over it."

To which our son Alex replied, "What are you talking about, Cath? Any bigger and you might have slums."

It is often compared to San Francisco, but having lived in San Francisco for years, I would think that this claim is surely an exaggerated stretch of the Kiwi imagination, as they are wont to do. Perhaps it might remind one of certain neighborhoods in San Francisco. Our apartment is near a Catholic monastery which towers over Oriental Bay and this area reminds me a bit nostalgically of the Filbert Steps area on Telegraph Hill, where Paul and I lived once upon a time in San Francisco. In my mind, there can be no other city to rival the beauty of the Golden Gate Bridge hanging over San Francisco Bay. But then I think of my most recent trip there a few months ago, tripping over all the ranting homeless people, the amount of rubbish on the streets, and people approaching me to sign petitions to impeach Obama.

As with the country itself, it's precisely what Wellington does NOT have which makes it a very attractive place to live.

The whole inversion thing in the southern hemisphere still stymies me at times even after all this time. Earlier this year while standing in line at the New World supermarket in Wellington with some Valentine treats in hand, I had one of "those" moments. Perhaps you are familiar with them? You know; the slightly disconcerting ones where the mind goes completely blank as you strive to make sense of what is before the eyes. In this instance, it happened to be a display of Cadbury's chocolate Easter eggs near the cash register. What had happened to me, I hope, was more of a Southern Hemisphere moment rather than a senior moment as

I stared fixedly at the stand, trying to comprehend why the heck Easter candy was out on display in the middle of summer. Was the store trying to hock inventory from last year or something like that?

Honestly, I was truly becoming a tad bit anxious, thinking this lapse was now real evidence that I was "losing it" at age fifty-seven. Abruptly, I forced myself to become orientated to place and time. What month were we in? February . . . summer here in New Zealand, and soon it would be March . . . with Easter following shortly thereafter, in what would be . . . eh, what? What's after summer . . . come on? Ah, not spring, but yes . . . autumn. That was it! And the season of autumn here, rather than spring, begins around March.

I still hadn't fully grasped or accepted the notion of Easter swapping seasons with Halloween. Easter is now experienced as a "fall" holiday, with the leaves changing all around me and various hues of orange, crimson and amber brown replacing soft, pastel spring colors. It is the pagan holiday of Halloween that now witnesses fragile spring blossoms with the hopes of warmer weather to come. Flipping summer for winter months was an adjustment as well, as firewood now had to be sourced around Christmas time and stacked by early April, and long dark nights endured from late April onwards til October.

It was only the summer temperatures here in December, January and February in the Southern Hemisphere which really didn't discombobulate me as much, as winter during those months in San Diego was always quite mild and sunny, so having a warm Christmas season was familiar enough. The difference was mostly felt in the amount of daylight hours we experienced at Christmas time in New Zealand that resulted in a noticeable dearth of outdoor Christmas lights, which we found ourselves missing very much. It doesn't grow dark until close to ten p.m., so it's rather pointless hanging outdoor lights around the houses, as one cannot fully appreciate the festive effects until close to bedtime. This is a land of mid-winter celebrations; with Christmas holiday-themed dinners and festivities held around the winter solstice in late June or early July.

Our second year here saw me digging out Christmas decorations at the end of June and stringing blinking lights outside the front of our house and in the bushes. Around forty guests showed up for my first mid-winter party, along with a few schoolmates from my children's schools. Roast turkey with all the trimmings, trifle and even a homemade Christmas plum pudding made by my new friend, Kasia, from Amsterdam adorned the festive table followed by much laughter as we played "naughty Santa" and haggled over gifts. Sadly, it's been a few years since I've hosted another mid-winter Christmas as I, along with many of my now empty-nester friends, try to escape to warmer climates during our winter.

And so it has been with much effort that I can now appreciate my son's birthday will be a chilly, wintery one in early July and that my birthday in January will occur in the middle of summer in this part of the world, while my daughter's special day in October is spring time and my husband has an autumn birthday in March. It's all switched around.

And now my daffodil bulbs are blooming in September, instead of April. Honestly, what am I doing here?

New Zealand Dreamin'

W HAT COULD POSSIBLY HAVE BEEN the impetus for such a drastic move, I am often asked by New Zealanders and foreigners alike. Did we have any connections here? Family? Work?

The answer to all the above is an emphatic no.

During that camping vacation in 2002, when we toured around both islands visiting all the usual tourist places in our motorhome—Rotorua, Taupo, Wellington, Picton, Blenheim, West Coast, Queenstown and ending in Christchurch—we wondered what it might be like to actually live in such a rugged and wildly beautiful country such as New Zealand. Upon our return home to San Diego, a certain restlessness, a certain "ennui" if you will, set into our psyche. This, along with the impact of a few well-timed words from a handsome young scientist from Tasmania whom I met at a campground kitchen outside Queenstown, had me thinking as well. He was in New Zealand doing research on the Franz-Joseph glacier and while chit-chatting over a cup of tea in the community kitchen, his response to taking on a new adventure or moving to a new country was, "Well, you know, it's not always what one DOES that one regrets, but often what one does NOT do."

Ummmm . . . OK.

There was another reason guiding my restlessness. I have to say that the day my twelve-year-old brother James walked out the front door of our house in rural Northern Ireland in 1972 and boarded a little red school bus not to ever return is the day I truly became aware of my own mortality. I was fourteen. He was killed instantly in a bus collision on a frosty February morning, Valentine's Day. To the relief of the other families, all the other children walked off the bus unscathed and soon wondered where my brother was when the head count was done. James was tragically the only fatality. Black ice, we were told, contributed to the skidding of one bus into the other on a curvy bend in the narrow country road. There was also talk that one of the drivers had been speeding, as he was running late and was under review for tardiness.

His taking the school bus that morning was in itself a fateful decision. Normally, he would get a lift from our neighbor up the road from our house, a teacher at his school; this particular day, he took a notion to ride the bus. As it was Valentine's Day and I had a handful of cards to hand out to my secret loves over the day, I teased him about perhaps fancying someone on the bus, but sadly, this was never verified as I never saw nor spoke to him again. Every Valentine's Day from that day forward would always be tainted with memories of my brother's death.

Over the years since that wretched day, I have come to realize that his sudden death was actually the greatest gift ever given to me in that it made me acutely aware and mindful that I, too, may one day leave the house and not return. This mindset has influenced many life decisions and not in the least our move to New Zealand in 2004.

I suppose one could say we, as a family, were indeed very privileged just to have experienced the notion of "ennui" in our own personal circumstances. We were living what was considered by many to be an enviable lifestyle in San Diego—close to the beach, perfect weather, great friends, kids in good schools—but . . . somehow, all was not that perfect. What???

As much as we loved San Diego, millions of others did as well and more and more people were relocating there every year. When we moved to Encinitas from San Francisco in the mid-1980s, there was no rush hour traffic to speak of and plenty of open land, planted with fields and fields of gladiolas. It was also around that time that Los Angeles, and most of the USA for that matter, "discovered" San Diego and with that, the population, cookie-cutter tract housing developments, strip malls and highways grew by leaps and bounds every year.

Instead of just hopping into my car and heading downtown to San Diego, I had to think about the time of day and what that implied in terms of the traffic. A drive that used to take ten minutes to get across the city of Encinitas, where we lived in our former life, lengthened to taking well over a half hour. Getting around the entire county was becoming more and more irksome. In the end, I felt like a hamster trapped in a small cage spinning a wheel frantically with a sense of desperation and getting nowhere fast. We were living a rather hectic and vexing life in a cement suburban jungle and I missed the open, green country of my youth.

There had to be a different way to live our lives. At first, we thought Ireland might be a good choice, as I had lived there as a teenager with my family and had many extended family members whom I visited regularly and were very welcoming. After careful consideration though, my very thoughtful husband thought it might not be the best option as he felt I might get sucked back into old friendships and cliques and possibly become entangled in ongoing family dramas and Irish feuds. In his mind, it would not be a novel experience or an adventure. He also did not want to work within the NHS, which was showing signs of strain. In hindsight, it was very fortunate we did not settle in Ireland then at the height of the "Celtic Tiger" which lost most of its pounce a few years later.

Why not New Zealand? Paul suggested. We frequently and fondly rehashed all our wonderful experiences traveling around both Islands, and felt encouraged enough to start exploring the reality of maybe relocating and working there permanently, in the South Pacific. How many times have I heard friends talk about their fantasy to sell out and re-invent a whole new lifestyle for themselves, preferably somewhere exotic? Too many.

Often, I had thought back to our first day on holiday in New Zealand when, after leaving the rugby players to sleep it off at the campgrounds, we set out on the road. We drove out of the camp, parked the motorhome close by Devonport, a quaint seaside town, and took the ferry over to downtown Auckland to have a quick look before we headed down south. After all, this is where most of New Zealand lives, over one and a half million of New Zealand's population of around four million. Surely it must have something worth seeing.

The four of us strolled up Queen Street, then veered off to a small side street where I came across a lingerie shop. Fantastic, as I had left the only bra I had packed back in Tahiti. While the others took off to the bookstore next door, I strummed through the sale rack for something reasonable and not too over the top in frills. As I passed over my Visa card, I asked the shop girl where she might advise a tourist to go if they had only two hours or so to explore the city. She hesitated a moment before an Asian lady joined me at the counter.

"Forgive me; I couldn't help but overhear. You say you have only an hour or so?" she asked.

Within a few moments, after paying and gathering my family from the bookstore, we were piling into her Range Rover parked nearby and she was driving us up Queen Street with her daughter to the Domain Park, both of them enthusiastically pointing out sites along the way. She dropped us off in front of the Auckland War Memorial Museum with instructions to have a cup of coffee by the duck pond followed by a stroll down Parnell Street on our way back to the ferry building.

Let me tell you, a cup of coffee in New Zealand is not the familiar American drip coffee. New Zealand has a thriving coffee and café culture and its citizens just adore their espresso-based beverages. What the heck was a *flat white?* Paul and I both ordered a cappuccino and were immediately asked if we wanted chocolate or cinnamon.

"What? Well, what about both?" I asked the young girl, which threw her a bit off guard. Remarkable! We took our coffees and sat by a pond outside, watching ducks flitting about, quite content and totally unconcerned with us.

We all agreed that this encounter with a complete stranger would never have happened in San Diego without reasonable suspicion as to motive. Indeed, I was pressed to remember one rude person on our entire camping trip, but then again, we were dealing mostly with foreigners in the campgrounds. Time and time again, when we commented on the beauty of the country, we were warned from these well-meaning folk that immigration laws in New Zealand are very strict and prohibitive. In other words, don't even think about it!

So, how did we end up moving from our seemingly idyllic San Diego lifestyle to a rural farming town in New Zealand? In fact, the notion that one would want to leave San Diego voluntarily and move to Wairarapa seemed so preposterous to one of our son's teachers, he seriously queried our circumstance.

"Let me try to understand this, Alex." He began. "Your father is a general surgeon from San Diego, and you move to Wairarapa? And your name is Middle-Eastern? Hummmm . . . Are you, by any chance . . . uhhh, in the witness protection program?"

This speculation provided more than enough laughter at our dinner table that evening, and still brings a smile to my face when I think back to that moment. We joked that even if we were he'd surely be the last to know.

Witness protection program aside, I usually attempt to explain our drastic move to curious ears by admitting that Paul and I were probably having a classic mid-life crisis, where one goes for either the new house, new car or new spouse, etc. Well, for better or worse, we decided to keep the spouse part of the equation and trade in everything else, including the country, for a dramatically different lifestyle.

Paul himself was growing quite weary of the whole U.S. healthcare system with its increasingly complex and faulty insurance schemes. He was discouraged with the dwindling autonomy and independence that American doctors once enjoyed practicing their art. He was working longer hours with less reimbursement and paying exorbitant malpractice insurance fees as a lawsuit lodged by a potentially disgruntled patient was constantly a very real threat. The focus was always on productivity, cramming as many patients into a clinic as possible. He was becoming disillusioned and deeply frustrated with only two weeks paid annual vacation to recharge his batteries.

Every surgeon around him was saying the same thing in so many words: they were fed up, disheartened and wanted to try something different. Some quit their jobs in large cities, and moved to places like Idaho or Colorado, but faced the same issues there and eventually returned to California. It's not always pragmatic or indeed an easy task to quit one's job as a surgeon, which involves years of specialty training, and re-train for something else.

Moving to New Zealand would be a true adventure in that we would be pioneers arriving in new territory with no friends or familial supports. Already there was evidence of a shift beginning, not only in hemispheres, but also in my marital relationship. I was usually the one to jump headfirst and impulsively into most things, while Paul played the devil's advocate and carefully stewed on the facts before committing to anything.

I might have inferred from family and friends when we were in the thick of planning that it was I who was driving this wild and impractical notion to move from the USA, and once again the more level-headed Paul would sit back and let me pursue this madness until I ran out of steam and then it would all just die down. But no, for the first time in our marriage, I had to hold back and let Paul assume the bulk of responsibility, as he being the major wage earner had to source a medical recruiter, chase down letters of reference and surgical logs, and ultimately have enough confidence in himself and his skills to be accepted and registered as a competent surgeon overseas. The last thing I wanted was for him to feel pushed or forced into this major decision and then come back at me filled with resentment and regrets. Indeed, as I witnessed him maneuver and navigate his way through New Zealand medical registration and secure a job, I fell in love with him all over again.

The seed to relocate thus planted, I set about doing some of the other busy work and fact-finding, with the first port of call being New Zealand immigration, which was rightfully considered the biggest hurdle to jump. Every traveler and prospective immigrant we had met during our brief holiday in New Zealand had lamented the difficulties encountered while trying to move there permanently. I rang the New Zealand immigration office in Washington D.C., and soon all the pamphlets and applications arrived in the mail, the fine print of which I pored over for at least a week.

There were a few suggested routes to obtaining a resident's visa back then. Age was an important factor, with preference given to those under fifty years, and having a confirmed job offer was crucial to speeding up the process. If one had over a million dollars to deposit into a New Zealand bank and let it sit there untouched for a couple of years was another route, along with starting a business and offering employment to local inhabitants. We applied under the needed professions guidelines as there were a few opportunities to apply for work as a rural general surgeon posted on the immigration website.

It was not long before I knew the staff at the New Zealand Consulate in Washington, D.C. by first name, and began ticking off the requirements on the application: FBI police certificates for each one of us, a complete health check with blood testing for HIV and syphilis, along with a signed medical certificate certifying that the family was in good health. Pictures had to be taken to an exact standard and notarized by a local solicitor or judge certifying that we were who we said we were. Towards the end of 2003, after much patience and persistence throughout the year, I rang my contact at the NZ Consulate in Washington D.C. to verbally verify that all was in order before I popped the application and documents in the post, only to be informed that NZ immigration was initiating an entirely new process beginning 1 January 2004, based on points, and our application would therefore be invalid.

"What?" I screamed into the receiver. "I've spent the better part of this year getting everything in order, dotted and signed, and now you're telling me it was all for naught?"

An "expedited" new application was promised to me; undaunted, I began the process once again of contacting the FBI for updated police files and made new appointments with our family physician to have the medical certificates updated with more bloods drawn. I also made trips back and forth to the bank to get money orders as preferred payments to the various U.S. and NZ government agencies. Our goal was to leave the USA shortly after the 2004 school year had finished, and after our son had obtained both his Eagle Scout award and his driver's license on his sixteenth birthday on 9 July.

The kids were very excited and every day after school, our thirteen-year-old daughter, Catherine, would ask had we heard anything from the New Zealand embassy or were there any updates about a job for Paul in New Zealand. At no time was there a moment's hesitation from either child. It was truly a family decision to relocate to New Zealand and begin a new adventure. As for our friends and family, I think our designs to leave our life in San Diego were initially not taken that seriously. How many times had they complained about escaping American politics, urban congestion, the illegal alien issues and the healthcare system and move somewhere else? Many, but then they would immediately offer a litany of excuses when asked, "Why not do it?"

I would have to say there were a couple of fateful occurrences upon returning from our holiday in New Zealand that enabled us to confidently make the decision to change our lives. Shortly before we took off on our South Pacific vacation a fixer-up house closer to the beach in Encinitas came on the market in exactly the area I had dreamed about owning a house one day. With the assistance of an agent, I made an offer and took off to Tahiti a few days later while it was being considered. We returned from New Zealand only to find out that we had been out bid by only $10,000, which in the grand scheme of things in Southern Californian real estate, was pennies. Something did not quite add up and the house was sold out from under us. Had we bought that house, we most certainly would not have moved as we would have been financially stretched at that point.

The other determining factor would have had to be our families.

How did we feel about leaving behind our families? And what about our aging parents? In my case, aging divorced parents had chosen to move from other parts of the country to live close to me. Me? Yes, me. Back then, things were not all that great in my family and a painful stalemate ensued amongst my siblings when my solution to our mother's ongoing health issues was largely ignored. As a result, it was with great frustration I witnessed my mother's condition decline rapidly, both mentally and physically, in her own house about twenty minutes from where I lived in Encinitas. I was working full-time then and would pop in to visit her between appointments. She had stopped taking her anti-depressive medications and was living on little more than cigarettes and tea. Despite my pleas and frequent reports on her condition, I really don't believe that any of the others in the family truly knew, or wanted to know, how badly off she really was at that time.

In the end, they all came rallying around, but it was an intervention of too-little, too-late. A hitherto very active and energetic paraplegic from a tragic fall twenty years earlier, she had developed huge pressure sores on her buttocks from lack of activity and lack of will to do much about it. When she was well enough, her house was put on the market, and with the blessings of my siblings, our mother went to live with my younger sister in the Midwest instead of with me. It was very generous of my sister to offer her house and services to our mother, but in the end I couldn't help feeling abandoned, helpless and rejected. Now I had no real reason to stick around San Diego.

My father, on the other hand, was then living in a very comfortable and very expensive assisted-care living complex around the corner from me that could boast once having Dustin Hoffman's father as a resident. Even with my negotiating a reduced monthly rate of $6,000 USD a month, my father's financial resources would hardly last two years at this facility as it only accepted cash. I had worked out an arrangement with the director and Paul and I agreed to top up the monthly balance with our own funds. He seemed to be as happy as was possible for him to be and was getting along well, in spite of his fluctuating mental and physical health.

No one else in my family bothered with him much for probably very valid personal reasons of their own, which again left me feeling resentful and angry. Being the eldest of eight children, I had had enough of him and his drunken antics in my childhood. I found it an ongoing struggle to feel a genuine love and concern for him, given our less than perfect and complex father-daughter relationship in the past. He had made some very unfortunate choices in his life and I had to remind myself that his current situation was not MY fault. His second wife of twenty years had left him a few years back and now he was alone. To be honest, my emotional resources were all dried up as far as he was concerned. It was clearly time for someone else to take the helm and oversee his affairs in my absence but there were no takers. It was now my time to fly the coop in a sense, as everyone else had already done without reservations. I was finished.

As for my in-laws . . . well, they lived in San Francisco and as I'd reminded my husband over the years, when one considered the little time and efforts they made to visit us and their grandchildren in San Diego, well, we might as well have been living in New Zealand. They were in their mid-sixties and enjoying life as well they should and deserved. They were always on the go with frequent trips to London, Europe and the Far East. They loved us dearly but were very busy in their own lives. They were more involved in their three daughter's lives and their children simply by default of proximity.

We figured even though New Zealand was on the opposite side of the globe and seemed so very far away, it took, in fact, the same amount of time to get there roughly as it would to Rome from California. Not too bad at all and, hopefully, our move would provide opportunities for our friends and family to visit and explore a new part of the world. I may sound very selfish and self-absorbed, but this is how I rationalized whatever guilt I was harboring about our impending change of life circumstances.

In order to get a reality check on practical aspects of life there, such as housing, schools, prices of things such as appliances, and to investigate job offers, Paul and I thought it wise to revisit our soon-to-be new country and planned a reconnaissance trip back to New Zealand in March 2004. We had thought Auckland would be our destination as Paul, practicing as a general surgeon, would have more opportunities for work situated nearer a large city.

But fate intervened once again when one of our neighbors encouraged me to get in touch with her former high school friend, Pam, who had been living in New Zealand, outside Wellington, for over twenty years. Pam was most helpful in that she immediately discouraged us from moving to Auckland.

"Trust me," she began, "if you are moving from Southern California to get away from traffic, congestion, and high prices, Auckland in not the place to go! Wellington has a much better public transport system and is the cultural capital of the country as well. The theatre, plays, opera, and not to mention the rugby; it's all-great here. It has more of a feel of San Francisco to it, whereas Auckland is more L.A., you know? Look, you're very welcome to come stay with me and check it out, OK?"

I immediately changed gears and booked a flight to Wellington for a week in March, around Paul's birthday. By that stage, Paul had been in contact with a medical recruiter, and appointments were being lined up while we were in New Zealand. The decision to fly to Wellington and base ourselves in the area proved most fortuitous, as the New Zealand Society of General Surgeons were holding their annual meeting that year in Martinborough, renowned pinot-noir wine country, an hour or so north of Wellington. This led to some important introductions during our short visit that enabled us to get some concrete leads on positions for Paul. Things really did seem to be working in our favor.

Living Amongst the Vines

THIS IS IT. HOLY JESUS, I cried, shielding my head and face from the sound of rapid gunfire. It's all going to end in a vineyard for me. And here I am totally sober. Isn't that the way of life? Lord help me!

We decided to base ourselves at a B & B in the quaint town of Martinborough to explore the Wairarapa area and to consider one of the current openings for a general surgeon at Wairarapa Hospital. It was crisp autumn weather in mid-March, the trees and grapevines glistening in various shades of gold and maroon as the potent New Zealand sunlight streamed through the high cloud cover. Paul and I had decided to take a walk early one afternoon through the vineyard behind our cottage when we became unexpectedly enveloped, to say the very least, in what appeared to be a shooting crossfire. Boom, boom, boom. Reload. Boom, boom . . . . Thoughts of Columbine and other senseless, horrific U.S. shootings flooded my mind as I crouched down on my hands and knees behind a vine, arms covering my head, fearing for my life as gunshots sounded around us. Oh my God! Was there some deranged madman out there trying to kill us for trespassing?

"What is going on?" I yelled to Paul, shaking uncontrollably. Scenes from any number of Vietnam War films flooded my thoughts as I dodged gunfire, truly! Soon we heard the sound of a motor vehicle humming towards us and I gingerly glanced around to see a man with a rifle slung over his shoulder driving a quad-bike straight at us. Paul gently put his arm around my waist as I held my hands up high, utterly defenseless and scared out of my mind. I had no idea what to think, when instantly the young man smiled at us.

"G'day! No worries. I heard there were two American guests going for a stroll out here and just wanted to warn you not to be alarmed." Then, after a rather long awkward pause and a wide smile, "It's the birds I'm after."

"What? What are you talking about? Couldn't there be warning signs or something put up?" I wailed as Paul pinched my waist to stop a potential hysteric tirade.

Well, he began to explain, this was the time of year, just before harvest, when the birds feasted on the grapes if the vines were not netted. The constant "shooting" we had been hearing during our walk was actually the sound of a purpose-built machine, propelling loud blasts of air into the vines to scare off the birds. He assured us that we were safe and free to roam around, and would not be shot at as he helped the machine do its job.

Oh, really? Uh, no, thank you very much. Completely frazzled at this point, I looked around for the nearest exit from the vineyard and gratefully hit the paved road back to our B & B. There, I threw myself on the bed with a huge tumbler of wine in an effort to calm my nerves after what I thought were to be the last minutes of my life on a leisurely walk through the vines. And yes, the absurdity of sipping wine after being scared out of a vineyard was apparent to me.

Autumn is clearly not the time to do this, trust me!!

This second visit to New Zealand forced me to see the country more in the light of actually living there, rather than being on holiday, a reality check. An area of the country had to be decided upon on where to live and set up a home. Paul and I had made some appointments with real estate agents to look at various properties in the Wairarapa area, north of Wellington. We wanted some land, preferably with a view and a sense of space, and maybe even build a house, something we had been priced out of in the San Diego market. One thing was certain:

New Zealand was not short on expanses of open, unpopulated land at relatively affordable prices. There seemed to be so much potential, so many fantasies to be fulfilled. After all, sheep do not require million-dollar views.

When I returned home from our short fact-finding mission, our children wondered why I was not jumping up and down with enthusiasm over the planned move. It was with more pragmatic thought and a sense of realism now that our plans and energies were fully directed towards the relocation. Everyone knows there is no utopian paradise on earth, and with more penetrating and objective observances, New Zealand was slowly unfolding itself as not the totally clean and green heaven-haven portrayed in travel brochures. This was reinforced by the immediate knowledge that New Zealanders in my son's class were elated that their family had succeeded in getting green cards in the United States Lottery and could thus continue to live in the US.

"It sort of makes me wonder," confided Alex that day when he came home from school. "This kid was so excited to be living here in San Diego, and here we are planning to move to New Zealand. What's up with that? And what's a green card?"

The country most assuredly did have some skeletons in its closets. Still, with confidence, I felt we were doing the right thing.

In 2004, the housing market in San Diego, along with the rest of California, continued to rise substantially in price. Our initial intention was to rent out our house, as we knew once it sold, we would not be in the financial position to buy it back. Sometime around April of that year, three months before we moved, we had the nagging intuition to sell. Paul and I thought it best that if we were going to take the plunge, we might as well do it full on and not have a foot in each country as it were. Selling our house would give us a stronger motivation to adapt to New Zealand life. The house was put on the market for what we thought was an exorbitant price, and to our astonishment, we had three full-price offers the first day, two of which fell through within a week.

After a bit of haggling, a sale was negotiated with a lovely young couple and a long sigh of relief.

Meanwhile, Paul was carefully considering a few job offers that had been proposed to him since our March visit to New Zealand. At the time, Greymouth was actually a serious contender, as we liked the idea of being on the west coast of the South Island. The resident full-time surgeon and his wife living there, whom we had met on an interview in Wellington, were most welcoming and described a rather bohemian-type community. When we had driven through this area close to a couple of years prior, it was glorious in its rawness and sunshine, with surfers tossing about in the dazzling blue, very empty ocean. I had yet to learn this was probably one of the rare days it had shown itself so well. Our new Kiwi friend Pam, however, vehemently discouraged this plan, describing the isolation and usual bad weather as major deterrents. In our ignorance, we perceived otherwise, and a few days before Paul had to sign his contract with the Greymouth District Health Board, our son went on the computer and did a Google search of Greymouth.

Within five minutes, another fateful event occurred when Alex swung around on a chair in our San Diego lounge, looked over at us in dismay and said: 'Hey guys, I'm really starting to re-think our move to New Zealand."

"What?"

"I'm reading here about Greymouth, and do you know how much it rains there?'

I immediately asked him to look up the annual rainfall in Galway, Ireland, where he had recently visited family of ours. He looked it up, and sure enough, it had more of an average annual rainfall. But his protests continued.

"Galway is gorgeous, and it's a university town. Lots of culture. And music. And it's Ireland, of course. Next door to Europe. Have you seen these pictures of where you want to live? Look here. This is Greymouth on a good day. And who would call a place Greymouth anyway? Grey MOUTH. It says it all." He pointed to the pictures on the computer screen. "I just don't think I can do this. Really."

And so, our lives were to be redirected once again in an instant. We were at this stage too far along in our mental and physical commitment to relocate to New Zealand to put a sudden halt to it, with our house and cars sold and Paul's resignation accepted. But this was the first serious objection from one of our children. It had to be addressed.

The next evening when we cuddled up on the couch and watched the film, *Whale Rider*, my daughter started in on us as well. "Is that the type of house we'll be living in over there?" She began. "It looks really poor and backward. I mean, look at their clothes! I don't want to go now. Nope."

Momentarily struck with panic, I turned to my husband and said, "What about that other job offer you had? The one in Wairarapa?"

"I thought you said you would live anywhere, but surely not there."

Somewhat reluctantly, my mind flashed back a few seconds to the dilapidated old hospital building through which we toured a few months prior, which has since been replaced by a beautiful new building, and some shabby-looking folk milling about the place, a few of them in patient gowns and Ugg boots huddled out front under the hospital eaves smoking, despite the poster-sized declarations that this was a Smoke-Free Zone.

I remembered clearly a young, very pretty girl in her late teens, walking back and forth with a baby stroller, trying to comfort the young child as it cried loudly and thrashed about in its seat. She was quite tall and wore a denim jean skirt that barely reached mid-thigh and a long white shirt that was opened over a pink tee shirt underneath. Her long, dark hair was brushed off her face and fastened behind her ears with small hair clips, highlighting her high cheekbones and fully exposing her light brown Māori complexion and dark brown eyes, one of which was darkened a deep purple from her eyebrow down to her cheek bone. Her gaze looked far into the distance as she methodically rocked the stroller back and forth and I could almost imagine her dire circumstances, trapped in an abusive relationship with nowhere to escape. What would this lovely girl's life hold in store for her had she been born in San Diego instead of Wairarapa? It all seemed a little bit too authentic for me at the time. But I had to be positive.

"Well, hey. It's got things going for it. It's near Wellington. And it has a pretty park . . . and it's wine country! Pinot noir. Lots of it. Hell, it can't be all that bad, huh? We'll make it work. It'll be OK. Really."

The next day, Paul was on the phone to the medical director we had met on our second trip in Wairarapa and serious contract discussions were underway. Pam gave me a list of the schools in the area and I started making enquiries to the principals and getting things lined up for admittance in late July 2004. Movers were secured, flights booked, and it wasn't long before going-away parties were organized by friends and neighbors. Everything hinged on getting our work visas from Washington, D.C. and Alex passing his driver's test on his sixteenth birthday and having a successful interview by an esteemed panel of judges to be granted the highest award in the Boy Scouts: Eagle Scout.

Alex and Paul had put in a few dedicated years into the Boy Scout experience, and it would have been a pity not to take it to its pinnacle. He needed the encouraging prod from us to get him over the finish line; in the end, he got his project sorted and completed in time, then successfully passed his interview two days before we moved. Only three percent of Boy Scouts in the United States ever make it to Eagle Scout, so that in itself would make this a prestigious honor for him.

Paul drove Alex to the Department of Motor Vehicles in our town the day before we were to fly out of L.A., and it was discovered that my car taillight had to be repaired before Alex could take the road test in that car. Frantic, off they ran to a service station where my husband practically begged a mechanic to do the repairs, then drove back to the department of motor vehicles only to be told the queue was now too long, and they would have to make another date. This not being possible, as we were flying out the next afternoon from Los Angeles, they sat there all day, and somehow managed to squeeze into the last appointment and thankfully, Alex passed his California driving test. Whew! Happy 16th Birthday! This was important as he would have had to do all the first-time driver requirements over again in New Zealand, and aside from giving him a bit more independence, it would save him time and us, yet more expense.

The farewell parties were many and bittersweet in the sense we were leaving so many memories and good friends behind as we confirmed our final details. Many were curious and openly envious of our decision to pack it all in for something different, so far away. Why couldn't we just relocate within the United States, say Montana, if open space and lack of people was ultimately what this sudden upheaval was all about? Sure, we considered that, but in the end we wanted a different way of life, with different accents, different politics and a total immersion in a distant English-speaking culture.

We listened to many and varied explanations, apologies and excuses from our friends as to why they would never embark on such a life-changing journey including: We have kids in good schools here. What about our cat and dog? We love our house; we have kids going to high school in AP courses, and how could they be uplifted? Maybe we should consider something like this after the kids are finished with college. I would lose out on my pension; I am contributing to my 401K and am at the height of my earning potential; I have too many friends and family here; I have aging parents; I would never find a job; and on and on it went. What were they thinking? What? That we too hadn't shared the same concerns, even more perhaps? But we persuaded ourselves, perhaps naïvely, that all would work out in the end. It was a case of blind faith in us, and in God.

Around that time, my sister's husband was doing risk analysis projections for corporate takeovers of large companies, and volunteered to do a risk analysis on our proposed move to New Zealand, taking into careful consideration such factors as our ages, the age of our children, current vs. projected income, etc. When he finished, it was not exactly what I had hoped to hear, i.e., taking all things at hand into account, he predicted we would last no longer than eighteen months. The reasons he proffered included the fact that my husband being of the age of maximum earning power, he would be throwing away precious years working as a surgeon in Southern California and saving for retirement. It was predicted our teenage children would probably "flip out" after the novelty wore off, and they would mostly miss their friends and the sunny, beachy San Diego lifestyle . . . and he assured us we would not want to live with disgruntled teens. Finally, he believed I would probably be bored to tears, having traded in my trendy and fun-loving neighbors and friends for insular, small town farmer's wives. What, no more happy hours at sunset by the beach? No blenders churning out frozen margaritas in my kitchen? Ouch! This did not sound promising at all!

A business associate of Paul's referred us soon thereafter to another American family from San Diego who had relocated to New Zealand a few years prior. I made contact with them by e-mail and soon we set up a telephone conference to discuss their experience as Americans living "down under." They first wanted to ascertain our reasons for moving from the United States, and why to New Zealand in particular. I sensed from their tone a certain guardedness and hesitation in their enthusiasm to encourage us in our decision to "sell out."

"You must know, it is very different here. It's the farmers who are the rich in this country. There is also a huge drinking culture here as well, and one of the highest rates of teenage suicides and pregnancies in the western world. I would say it takes a good three years living here before you feel that you are truly living here, and not going back to your bed in the USA. The first year you still have the feeling that you are on vacation, as everything is still in the discovery stage with new living circumstances, settling in, what have you. The second year it begins to dawn on you that, hey, we're not in Kansas anymore. It's only in the third year that you will know you are here to stay. If you do stay that is. We know a few families that have packed it all in, and have either moved back home or on to Australia. I met someone who didn't even wait until his container was unpacked to make up his mind. He had it turned around at port and flew himself and family back home to Colorado I think. Hey, I don't mean to put the kibosh on your plans, but I just want you to have a clear picture of what you're getting yourselves into."

Not very encouraging overall, but we as a family of four took this input onboard and, undaunted, we still decided to hold hands and together jump off the USA country pier to try something completely different.

Two nights before we were to leave our neighborhood, our friends joined forces and hosted a festive farewell pizza party at our community pool. We were presented with a photo album filled with a diverse collage of events over the past seventeen years we had spent amongst them, encompassing birthday parties, christenings, graduations and other celebrations. There were many questions about the logistics of our imminent move and the cultural aspects of New Zealand, which led me to infer that amongst them very little was actually known or appreciated about our soon-to-be-adopted country. I tried to answer a few of their questions as best I could, considering my own limited knowledge of its history and social mores. Do the natives dress in their costumes regularly? What kind of food do they eat? Can you take a ferry over to Australia, and how long would that take?

Do you need a passport to go back and forth to Australia? New Zealand has TWO islands? One of my closest friends leaned into me and actually asked, Hey, by the way, do they speak English down there?

Mind you, these musings were coming from folk who could boast quite a few stamps on their U.S. passports and considered themselves quite well traveled and educated. Honestly!

I could only imagine the thoughts going through my father's head as he sat alone at a table and sullenly observed all the hugs, kisses and even tears. We were the envied and celebrated lot, the one's escaping crowded Southern California to far away adventures at the bottom of the earth in enchanting and mystical New Zealand.

I joined my father and assured him we would stay in constant communication, that direct debits were all in place to pay his rent, and he would have enough funds to maintain his current lifestyle. He was very saddened to be losing his only support, and I had to forge through my personal guilt and carry on with the plans set in motion.

A week later, professional movers arrived with a forty-foot container truck and assured me they would have it packed in less than two full days. As this was an international move, I was not permitted to pack anything, as every item had to be logged for customs. After all, if not monitored, who's to know if illegal drugs or arms were being packed amongst contents? So, while my husband and son were off in New Mexico fly-fishing as was promised for his sixteenth birthday–lucky them–I watched over six burly men as they took my house hostage and, room by room, wrapped and packed while I tried to answer as best I could the frequent queries: "Hey, you taking this? You taking that?"

As I had just quit working full-time as a medical case manager the previous week, I never got around to putting the yellow sticky tabs, as requested, on things I didn't want to bring over to New Zealand; for example, most of the electrical appliances. In the end, drawers filled with whatever items were literally dumped into boxes before I could go through them and filter through seventeen years of hoarding. It was both heart wrenching and totally draining to watch over all this methodical, insensitive packing and witness my life in that house vanishing before my eyes, being reduced to perfunctorily labeled cardboard boxes. The impermanence of it all, of life itself, struck me hard at that moment. What had been my life in that house for over sixteen years now felt like a scripted set being pulled down to make way for the next set, to be newly scripted and played by different actors.

In any case, it would be at least six months before I would revisit the treasures and possessions of my San Diego life.

When the last items were hoisted up into the truck, I stared in almost disbelief as the doors were forcefully pushed closed, locked, and driven off to the Los Angeles Port for departure sometime that week. I turned around in the driveway and walked slowly towards my vacant and empty house, now mostly devoid of all signs of our life there. A thorough house cleaning had been planned for the next day, and before I locked up, I walked upstairs and bid farewell to the three bedrooms. There I stood before each one, remembering happy times passed rocking babies to sleep, telling bedtime stories, playing board games, decorating Christmas trees for the kids at the foot of their beds, escorting close friends to the spare room when they had over-indulged, and greeting each morning from the balcony outside my bedroom, looking out to the Pacific Ocean.

Yes, it had been a very happy house, and in it, I was truly blessed. The new owners, a lovely young couple, would shortly fill these rooms with their treasures and make their own wonderful memories. I said thank you to each and every room and space, and then I drove over to a friend's house close by, where we were to spend our last night in Encinitas, and promised myself that soon I would have the well-deserved luxury of doing nothing, longing only to stare at fields of sheep from a window in my New Zealand home.

Our last stopover took us to Long Beach, where our stay in Southern California had begun almost twenty years prior, to visit our dear friends Kim and Marianne, who lived in the same house where we had our wedding reception. A colorful paella, pitchers of margaritas, and a festive bon voyage cake was enjoyed, along with many promises to visit us in our soon-to-be adopted home. Giddy with excitement and anticipation, I hugged Marianne tightly and then we were whisked to L.A.X airport with our one-way circuitous ticket to Wellington, New Zealand with a few carefully planned detours en route via the Cook Islands, Sydney, the Gold Coast and Melbourne, Australia. As Paul had never taken more than two weeks off in a row on a vacation, this was the time to do it, before he became entrenched in his new appointment as Consultant General Surgeon at Wairarapa Hospital. We were on our way, and with one last look down at the gridlocked L.A. freeways from the jet plane window, I switched off my American cell phone for the last time, and closed my eyes from sheer exhaustion.

Shrimps on the Barbie

THE COOK ISLANDS PROVED A most welcome and hard-earned respite from the hectic pre-move months, which largely remain a bit of a blur to this day. The Cook Islanders were warm, the resorts unpretentious and the island small enough to navigate around on a scooter. After four days there, we left the relative warmth and relaxed island pace and flew into Sydney to stay with some UK friends we had met the previous Christmas in Patagonia, South America.

Julie and I had sealed our friendship when she helped me close the bar on a small ship one night when both our families were traveling through the Magellan straits and around Cape Horn. At that time, she and her husband were in the process of emigrating from London to Australia, so we had much to talk about as we were almost at the same stage ourselves with our application to New Zealand. She had moved to Sydney only three months ahead of us and had already bought a house in Paddington, had her six-year-old daughter enrolled in a top-notch private school and had found part-time work with a marketing firm. Her husband was still conducting his business in Europe from Australia; so all seemed to be going very well for them. She was the source of much support and encouragement to me during the angst-ridden months before the actual move. It could be done, she promised.

The four of us landed on their doorstep, carting the maximum allowed checked luggage per person—two bags weighing thirty-two kilograms each, along with a few carry-ons and a surfboard in tow. I'd say it must have been a bit overwhelming for the rather sedate British husband, but the "Irish" part of the equation, Julie, was unperturbed. That evening, it was pleasant enough to sit outside with the barbecue fired up, and soon large prawns were tossed on the grill.

"I can't believe it! This is too funny." I called out in my best Crocodile Dundee imitation: "So, they really do do shrimps on the barbie down here, eh?"

While I was walking with Julie around Centennial Park the next day, I asked her how she was *really* getting along in her new life in Australia. It was in that conversation that I first heard the term "pom," a term she uttered matter-of-factly when describing how Aussies sometimes treat immigrants from England. "You know," She began, "the Aussies don't really like us poms".

So, what's a pom?

She explained that the term pom was given to new British immigrants, more specifically the English as having just arrived from gloomy England, they did not protect themselves from the sun and became very sunburned which turned their fair skin red, resembling a pomegranate. Here in New Zealand, the term is usually prefaced with derogatory adjective such as "bloody" or "whingeing, as in, "He's a whingeing pom; what would you expect, eh?"

It's usually taken as a disparaging term, and dare I say, an ethnic slur? To be sure, British people consider the expression "pommy"—often shortened in true "Down Under" fashion to pom—somewhat offensive as used by speakers of Australia, New Zealand, including sometimes the English speakers of South Africa as well as the Afrikaans, despite the Australian Advertising Standards Board ruling in 2006 that the term is now not offensive.

I understand from my limited research on the expression pom that the origin of this term is really not confirmed and several false etymologies persist to date. The Oxford English Dictionary strongly supports the claim that pom did, in fact, originate from the word pomegranate, suggesting it is an extinct Australian rhyming slang for immigrant, as in Pummy Grant, meaning an assisted immigrant. There does not appear to be any hard evidence, though, for the theory relating to sunburn. People have since insisted to me that the term is an acronym for "prisoner of His/Her Majesty" or "prisoner of Mother England," as many of the first British settlers in Australia were convicts sentenced to deportation to Australia, often for menial crimes. Proponents of this theory claim that when the prisoners arrived, they would be given a uniform imprinted with "POHM" or "POME" on the back, which reportedly stood for Prisoners of His Majesty or Maidenhood Prison, but again, there are no images or records of these uniforms. As the term is still frequently used today in New Zealand to describe recent immigrants, I had assumed it meant that as a "Prisoner of Mother England," a POM was one unwilling to let go of England's customs and lifestyle. To date, no one has agreed with me on this interpretation.

In saying this, one of the biggest feathers in a New Zealander's cap is waxing lyrical about their glory days working and sharing flats in London while on their grand OE. What the heck is an OE, pray tell? As the Kiwis acknowledge their relative geographic isolation, it is part of their culture to take off on an extended trip overseas, and do their OE, an overseas experience. This is usually a working holiday and occurs a few years after university graduation and, as opposed to the British gap year, is self-funded once one has saved enough funds for airfare and lodging for a time. It can extend for a few months or for years as many Kiwis have dual citizenship through their parents.

London and eastern Australia both have sizable ex-pat Kiwi populations to date. Inevitably, many Kiwis fall in love overseas and, like the wandering albatross, return home to their "colony" to raise a family. It's rather confusing as Kiwis can be deriding the British in one sentence, as in "Pommy Bastard," then wax on and on longingly about their OE back in the mother country and their glorious London days.

I was reminded initially of the film *Gangs of New York*, where the character played by Daniel Day Lewis greets scruffy Irish folk fresh off the boat with a passionate vehemence when he pronounces himself to be distinctly American, having been born in the USA and first generation. He had no wish to be even remotely associated with this pathetic immigrant lot, even though his parents had emigrated from Ireland with the last generation.

Often we are asked, "Why New Zealand, and not Australia, for our big life-changing move?" To be honest, Australia was briefly considered, but in the end, we thought it too close to what we were leaving behind in San Diego. We were saying farewell to the best of beach and barbecue culture as far as we were concerned, and had no intention of emulating it with an Australian accent. Aside from which, our American television and media had been bombarded with Australian clichés such as heard and seen in *Crocodile Dundee*, along with Steve Irwin's antics, and there would have been unrealistic expectations on our part. Good or bad, we had no such expectations as far as daily life in New Zealand was concerned.

After a few more obligatory "baaahbies," lunch at Bondi Beach, ferry rides to Manly, and several photos of the iconic Opera House and Harbor Bridge (both spectacular sites), it was off north to Burleigh Heads to visit erstwhile friends from our former neighborhood who had settled on the Gold Coast. Our friend Brett had always wanted to return to his Aussie homeland, and finally got his San Diegan wife and children to acquiesce to his wishes. Our son was thrilled to be surfing without a wet suit on some of the most famous breaks in the world, while a few of us were lucky to spot migrating whales offshore.

Next on our meandering route to Wellington was Melbourne, where I had a cousin living from Ireland with her Aussie husband. We enjoyed all the ethnic food, the ease of public transport, the trendy shops and general buzz of this very cosmopolitan city. While dining on some authentic Middle-Eastern cuisine, we learned that Melbourne could boast the largest Greek population in the Southern Hemisphere. This catered to my husband's Armenian palate very nicely. Finally, it was with a bit of trepidation that we boarded the plane, leaving the sunny land of "shrimps on the barbie" behind, to fly across "the ditch," formally known as the Tasman Sea, to our new home: Wairarapa, New Zealand.

Getting Settled

THE MEDICAL DIRECTOR AND A secretary from the Human Resources department, with whom we had been in contact over the past few months through anxious e-mails and frequent phone calls, met us at Wellington International Airport and happily transported our luggage in a large van to the temporary home where we were to be planted for six months. They left us a car so we could spend our first night with our new friend, Pam, up in the west seaside town, Paraparaumu, on the Wellington "Gold Coast".

It took me months before I could properly pronounce the name of that city, which most locals refer to simply as Paraparam. New Zealanders are quick to abbreviate any word possible and it took some time for us to get accustomed to Kiwi slang. Australia is "OZ," the Tasman Sea is "The Ditch," Australians are "Aussies." In the Kiwi vernacular, breakfast becomes "brekky," gift is "prezzie," sparkling wine is either "champers" or "bubbles," afternoon is "arvo," and location becomes "pozzie." More to follow on this later . . .

Our warm hostess in Paraparaumu had invited her next-door neighbors over to welcome us for a typical Kiwi dinner of rosemary and garlic-studded roast lamb, oven-roasted winter root vegetables including kumara (which is what we knew as sweet potatoes in our former lives), parsnips, pumpkin, (not what we would have called pumpkin), carrots, beets and potatoes. Dinner was followed with a fresh cream-topped pavlova, adorned with sliced kiwi fruit and mandarins. All washed down with plentiful New Zealand wines.

We were then invited to take our seats in the living room before the television to watch South Africa play the New Zealand team, the All Blacks, in one of the Tri-Nation's final rugby games. I had no idea what all the yelling and cheering was about as I tried to make sense of the rugby game, but the enthusiasm in the room was infectious and I made a sincere attempt to join in as best I could while listening to explanations from Pam about what had just happened in the play. The most important rule for me to understand was that the ball is thrown backward, and not forward, as in American football. Okay . . . .

The next morning, Pam gave us each departing gifts of "polar thermal" brand gloves and hats. "You'll be needing these," she carefully cautioned. "It's colder, and damper, where you're going, it being a valley. And this has been a very cold winter. I reckon you're going to wish you had chosen the Gold Coast to live. The Gold Coast, Australia that is.

Wonderful!

On the way to our new home, over a very windy narrow pass in the Rimutaka hills, we drove through a few country towns, passing boutique-type antique shops, quaint clothing store windows, cafés and bakeries and a few buildings that looked like pubs. Many times we had the two-lane road—which is the major and only motorway going north through this valley from Wellington—all to ourselves. The sun was quickly ducking behind the rolling Tararua hills, casting a warm hue over densely native bush and green fields. Paddock after paddock of sheep could be seen grazing the empty expanses in between the towns and on the distant eastern hills.

"Wow! There's more sheep than houses over here," our daughter called out from the back seat.

"Yep! And that's a good thing," I answered.

"Do you think we could get a few sheep?" our son chimed in.

"Well, we can surely look into it."

"What?" Paul looked over at me.

"Hey, we made it this far, haven't we? Why not?" I answered.

"You're right. For better or worse, we're here all right. At the bottom of the earth." Paul smiled.

We arrived at our accommodation late that Sunday afternoon, after a quick stop in town to purchase some hot water bottles for the bed, as I had used way back in my teens during winter in Ireland. The rental house, situated only a few blocks from the hospital and walking distance to the town and nearby shops, proved an excellent location. I had prepared the children and myself for the worst, in terms of the comforts and indulgences we had left behind in San Diego, and thus we were pleasantly satisfied with the house the hospital provided for us. It had everything we would need in the way of cooking supplies and general appointments.

The couple who owned the house were both school teachers and had taken up a post in the UK for a year, so the house was rather "homey" and not sterile as a hotel or condominium rental might have been had we been placed there. We immediately lit the fire in the living room and, after turning on the individual room heaters in the bedroom, the chill was soon off the house. The refrigerator had been stocked with all the ingredients to make spaghetti Bolognese, along with a six-pack of beer, two bottles of wine and some local sheep's milk cheese. What more could I possibly want? It was all that was needed at that time to feel at home.

The next morning, we were awakened to a loud knocking on the front door. There the medical director stood, looking somewhat solicitous.

"Soooooo, how was your first night then?" he hesitated.

"Great. We lit a fire, had dinner and packed in early," Paul smiled back.

"You weren't too cold then? It was one of the coldest nights to date last night, or so it was reported this morning. Was the firewood dry?"

"What do you mean? Dry? It seemed to burn OK and, well, we slept just fine," my husband assured him, as he looked around the yard and marveled at the beauty of the snow-capped mountains in the distance.

"Did you have the electric blankets on, then?"

"No, we didn't know about them." I answered. "We filled up the hot water bottles and they did the trick." To be sure, once the electric blankets were discovered, the hot water bottles were quickly put to rest in the linen closet.

The first order of the day was to contact both the schools and make the necessary appointments with the principals, or headmaster and/or headmistress. As the New Zealand school year had just started back again after the mid-winter break, I was anxious to get my two children on track as soon as possible, while Paul went to the hospital to begin the paperwork and orientation required before he could practice there.

The next day, we dressed in our finest and drove a few kilometers north of town to the boy's private high school, "college" in New Zealand. The road leading to the school was studded with sheep and cattle. Once inside the school gates, the grounds were indeed impressive in its bucolic setting, reminiscent of a posh American East Coast prep school. The school buildings scattered around the gentile campus were ivy-clad character structures with a distinct English feel about them. The all-boys school— which in the last two years has become co-ed—was highly recommended to us by my friend Pam and others at the hospital and we hoped Alex would make a good impression. With some trepidation, we followed the signs for the office, where we were asked to take a seat. The headmaster, dressed neatly in a suit and tie, walked out from his office and met us in the foyer.

"Would you like a cup of tea?" he asked immediately, before we sat down for what we had assumed would be a formal assessment. He gave the academic folder handed to him a perfunctory glance, nodding his head in the affirmative and then, to our bewilderment, he began quizzing Alex about the surfing breaks in San Diego. This at once put Alex at ease and lessened the sense of anxiety he might have perceived amongst us. It also provided a chance for him to assess how articulate Alex came across along with a sense of his personality; looking back at that moment, it was very clever of him indeed. After the short interview, he gave us a short walking tour of the campus that included viewing remnants of a small Greek-inspired amphitheater.

As it was mid-year, both our children were given the option to go forward in the age-appropriate year, or elect to remain a half a year behind their U.S. counterparts. Both decided to be placed forward, which rather worried me, as I had repeatedly warned them that New Zealand, assuming it to have modeled its education system on the UK, would be way ahead of U.S. standards.

I was rudely humbled at age twelve by my Irish peers at school in Northern Ireland, who were learning two or more foreign languages, memorizing stanzas from Shakespeare and working on math that was totally foreign to me. Coming from a private school in America, I had arrogantly assumed that I would be far ahead of those in my year, but this definitely was not the case. The next few months would test my concerns and very soon confirmed this was not to be the same experience for Alex and Catherine.

The headmaster warmly welcomed Alex as a new pupil and told him there was a daily bus service available with pick up from the local dairy in our area. *Dairy?* What did he mean by that? I had images of cows mooing away in straw-filled barns waiting to get milked somewhere near our house in town. What a strange place to have a school bus stop, I thought, but somehow it seemed to fit living in rural New Zealand.

Catherine was interviewed later that morning at the private girl's college across town from our house by the vice principal, a lovely, soft-spoken woman of Russian descent, as the principal was engaged that day. She questioned our motivations to move to the Wairarapa region all the way from San Diego and thoughtfully advised us that folk either truly fall in love with the area, or quickly don't. Then leave. Yikes! Which group would we fall into after settling in?

We were calmly assured that Catherine would be able to cope with the academic demands of being placed with the girls a year ahead. As was the case with Alex, the letters of introduction and academic standing from the American schools were barely acknowledged, never mind scrutinized, and a placement was offered to begin classes as soon as the uniforms were sorted the next day. We were escorted around the campus and were impressed with the air of decorum—and dare I suggest, chastity—the smartly dressed young girls personified as they walked briskly to and from classes.

Indeed, Catherine—kitted out in a long, pleated black skirt to just above her ankles, thick black opaque stockings, a grey shirt, striped tie, a grey wool V-neck jumper and a hip-length navy striped blazer-finished off with regulation black, lace-tied, chunky, male-looking shoes—was more modestly clad than most Catholic nuns back in the States. Good-bye to designer jeans, denim mini-skirts, shorts and tee-shirts which were the standard look at our local public San Diego high school. Gone also was the torment of daily wardrobe dramas along with hair styling; it had to be worn in a ponytail with a black (only black) hair tie, and no make-up, which was strictly forbidden along with earrings and other jewelry.

But, alas! This veil of propriety was abruptly lifted soon thereafter when a nurse at the local clinic in town informed me she felt compelled to inform the girls when giving a talk on sexual education that it was OK NOT to have sex. Sadly, the veneer of modesty and chastity, as suggested by the regulation uniform, was to become a bit of a joke in the months to follow, as tales of the local social teenage mores soon testified.

Getting ready for school the next morning now took some effort on Catherine's part as learning to knot the tie properly was quite taxing in itself. I won't bother going on and on about the testy complaints revolving around the efforts it took to divest oneself of the multiple layers of clothing to use the restroom in a hurry. Our son's uniform was rather straight forward in comparison in that he wore dark grey trousers, green shirt, striped tie, and a plain dark grey wool jersey over it all, with a blazer as well. This is very cool, he thought, saying he felt like a WWI soldier. And so, on one very frosty morning in late July with the snow-capped local hills as a backdrop, I drove both children to their respective campuses where everyone bustled about in the exact same attire. They belonged. Or so I had hoped.

Soon the experiences of rural New Zealand school life were being relayed to me on a regular basis, which brought home the stark and sobering reality that we were indeed in a different culture. Catherine had been invited to a local boy's fourteenth birthday party, the son of one of the staff at the hospital. The day before the party, she said she received a text message from the birthday boy—texting being something we were all trying to get our heads around as no one seemed to use their phones to actually make a call, citing the exorbitant expense—apologizing for the fact that his mother was forbidding alcohol to be brought to the party.

Why should that be an issue, I wondered, as this was gathering for a group of very young teens? Well, the drinking age in New Zealand was lowered from twenty years old to eighteen in 1999 and recent studies suggested that this was not a particularly good thing, in that the incidence of car crashes amongst the 18-20 years age group had markedly increased, as well as antisocial and disruptive behavior in this group. It is not uncommon for parents here to provide youngsters under eighteen with a few RTDs, those bottled sugary ready-to-drink mixed "cocktails," to take to parties and then allow these children to spend the night at the friend's house.

Despite pleas from my teenage daughter, I was grateful when a local South African parent warned me not to allow our children to spend the night at a party, as that was when all the trouble might begin in terms of excess drinking and unprotected sex. Let's just say it would not have been my idea of the traditional American sleepover, to say the least.

So, off we drove Catherine and a girlfriend to the party around 7 p.m. one Friday night and advised her that we want to collect her around midnight. We received a text around 11 p.m. asking could she please, PLEASE, stay there until 12:30 a.m. as the party was just beginning to liven up a bit, so I agreed that this was the absolute latest time I would drive out there, about ten minutes from town, to get her and heard nothing more. She and her friend were all giggles and whispers in the car ride home, and did not divulge too much, only saying it was really fun in the end.

During the course of the week, I had heard from one of the parents that the boy's mother went out regularly throughout the evening to the bonfire with a large torch (flashlight) to check that no one was drinking and to ensure everyone was behaving. When I mentioned this to Catherine, she cringed a bit and confessed it wasn't just the alcohol that was the primary concern, but the activity in the bushes.

"What do you mean?" I asked her?

"Well, it was sooooo obvious, Mom," she said, "that people were doing *IT* in the bushes".

"What? What do you mean by *IT*?"

"What do you think? Yes," she said, nodding her head up and down. "And, at one point a few of the kids yelled, 'Hey, we can see you in there. Humping.'"

I could not believe what she was telling me, and so matter-of-factly at that.

Apparently there was one young fellow who was visited by several girls at different times during the party for viewing and/or servicing in the bushes. Now, I'm painfully aware that teenage sex is prevalent at even junior high schools in California, but unless I am terribly naïve, I strongly doubt this would have happened at the home of one our friends in San Diego during a birthday party for a fourteen-year-old. Am I right?

A week later, Paul, Catherine and I drove Alex out to a community hall in the country for an eighteenth birthday party for a twin brother and sister in his class. Alex bought a card and asked us for some cash, $10 for each twin, as a present. He assured me this was plenty, as when he had asked friends about birthday presents, he was told just to bring some beer.

We drove along very dark, winding country roads about fifteen minutes from us when we came across this sole building in the middle of nowhere, literally. We knew we were in the right place when we saw groups of teens milling about outside, holding beer cans and RTDs in their hands and smoking. Alex begged to be dropped off a bit down the road from the party in the dark so it would appear we were not over-solicitous.

"Don't go in the bushes," Catherine called after him. I watched out the rear window as Alex strolled, a bit self-consciously I thought, with two birthday cards in hand towards a group by the front door and fought the memory of my brother-in-law advising me that we wouldn't last here longer than eighteen months. God help us!

The next week, Alex came home from school and asked me how I would define the concept of feminine to someone. "You see," he began to explain, "when I told this kid at school that I didn't think the girls in our year were very feminine, he didn't know what I meant; he said he thought they were all spot-on."

I thought for a moment. "Well," I began, "I think it's about a girl who takes pride in being a female, and likes to dress well to flatter her figure, might use perfume to smell nice, likes make-up a bit, and generally behaves in a manner particular to girls, to the female sex I suppose. Why?"

"Well," he faltered, "the girls at my school are, uh, so like guys. They fart out loud, curse all the time, and hardly anyone has long hair. When I tried to open a door for a girl last week, she got all huffy and yelled at me. 'What the fuck? You think I can't open the door myself?' I didn't know what to say.

I personally had noticed a certain lack of chivalry and thoughtfulness amongst the local New Zealand men I had recently come across, and a pronounced toughness and determination about the women here who could and did put their hand to anything a man would normally do around the house or land, reminiscent of the American prairie women. As a result of living so far away from another country, Kiwis have had to invent things they could not easily obtain. Their creativity and ingenuity is reflected in the use of No. 8 wire, a reference to a gauge of fencing wire which has been adapted for many other uses on the farm and at home, whereas Americans are noted for their reliance on duct tape.

Yes, most of the women here do not have long flowing locks or embrace plastic surgery, regular manicures or pedicures to the degree which some of my friends chasing youth back in San Diego were known, but I find this truly refreshing in that they wear their aging authentically and unapologetically. Truly, I receive many more compliments here than I do when I am back in the U.S. and generally feel better about myself overall. I accept the fact that I am aging, and will never return to the way I looked in my twenties, thirties or forties. Such is life.

But back to the men: usually back home when a man notices a woman struggling with groceries or heavy items, he is quick to approach and ask if she needs any assistance. After all, this is a gentleman-like thing to do, aside from being kind and thoughtful. Not so in this area. Many a time I could have used some help carting heavy items from various stores to my car. Perhaps the men were fearful they might actually offend a woman and thus be publicly denounced in the same foul-mouthed manner as my son had been. Then again, maybe I'm generalizing too much here in that this perhaps reflects rural vs. urban life.

I'm prompted here to digress a bit and muse about the New Zealand dating culture, or seeming lack of it, as gleaned from my teenagers over our years here and, most recently, from a local Kiwi comedian, Ben Hurley, in a skit which went something like this: "I met this friend at work from the States who was eager to meet some real nice Kiwi women. He asked me what I might suggest to do to really impress one, to which I answered, 'Mate, take her on a date. Now that's something a Kiwi woman wouldn't be used to, going on a date! Fish AND chips! This is a culture of drinking and rooting . . . . We get drunk and root. We wake up the next morning and look right, then look left and if she's still there we're with her for a few years."

Once, when I asked my son if he was seeing—as in dating— any nice girls up in Auckland University, he just shook his head in the negative. I soon infered that it was perhaps not the custom to go out with a girl a few times and then not see her again. Once one latches onto someone, that seems to be the end of dating, and many stay in the relationship even if they're unhappy and moaning and groaning about it. He told me about an American exchange student at his dormitory who went to a party with him a few weeks ago and got talking to a girl whom he fancied and all seemed to be going well. After a while, he asked her if she would like to go out to a movie the next night. She gave him the weirdest look and said, "Why would I go out with you? We don't even know each other".

Apparently, if he, and she especially, were to have gotten drunk and then ended up back at his or her place for a bonk, that would have been OK. Then she would have been happy to go out to a movie with him the next night. Go figure.

My heart went out to my son at that moment.

When my daughter was at university in Wellington, I learned that if one meets a prospective suitor at a bar or party, numbers are exchanged, then the texting begins, back and forth until an invitation is made to visit the other at their flat and ending up in the bedroom. A relationship can go on like this for months, back and forth to one another's flat with not so much as a drink at a bar, or a meal out, or a movie, i.e. no "date." Now I know full well that students are rather skint, but one could still manage a simple picnic in a park or a walk along some beach without breaking the bank. Catherine confided in me that she adamantly refused to go to a guy's flat, as the last thing she wanted was to sit on a couch, watch a DVD, then be felt-up . . . . No, she tells them, if you want to meet me, we have to DO something social, in public.

One has to be reminded that up until fairly recently, New Zealand was quite isolated in the world, which led to an insular mindset crowned with an air of suspicion. But this is changing rapidly; with more and more young folk traveling overseas, socialization skills have expanded and become more refined upon return.

Aside from some awkward attempts to assimilate as painlessly as possible, all went well enough during those first few weeks. We settled into a daily routine much like we had left behind in California during the school year. As it was winter with its long nights, we would light the fire early in the evening and, after dinner, watch television together, usually American shows, which was something I had not done back home. After having been recommended a few locally made films including *Once Were Warriors* and *The Price of Milk*, I had no further desire to watch more homespun stories about New Zealand life. In fact, I watched more American television in those first few months settling in to New Zealand than I had over most of my life as a parent. It seemed to bond us together as a family in our alien environment.

Our children seemed to enjoy their new schools and the rather short-lived celebrity status conferred upon them as Americans on campus. Once, I heard Alex singing what sounded like a hymn while showering, which was very unusual for him. To my knowledge, before our move he had never sang. He was singing loudly and with such fervor that curiosity got the better of me.

"What was that you were singing?" I asked him.

"Oh, it's one of our songs for the house music competition: 'You Raise Me Up.' We have to sing one religious hymn and one contemporary song. And I volunteered to be the conductor for our house as no one was putting their hand up."

What was he on about, I wondered? I had no idea what a house music competition was but learned that the boys were assigned to one of three houses at this school and often competed against one another in sports—very *Harry Potter*! What joy I had as a mother, watching him wearing formal tails and leading his house to victory while also earning the Best Conductor award. He was amazing! To this day, I smile with fond memories whenever I hear the hymn he sang along with their rendition of the Dave Dobbin song, "Slice of Heaven."

After a month or so at school, Alex came home one day and said he had met a girl in his class from San Diego. What a coincidence. Her family had moved to New Zealand ten years prior and she wanted to ask her mother to invite us over for dinner. It wasn't long before I, too, began receiving invitations from some of the doctor's wives at the hospital for morning tea, lunch, or drinks and nibbles to get to know some of the community. It was clearly time to put myself out there.

Once Were Warriors vs. Wharekauhau Estate

I HAD LIVED IN NEW ZEALAND only five minutes when my close friend Carol from San Francisco rang me and asked, "So what's it really like living there? *Once Were Warriors* or Wharekauhau Estate?"

"I have absolutely NO idea what the heck you are talking about."

"Haven't you seen that film *Once Were Warriors*? It was out in the early '90s. It's set in New Zealand and all about their native culture."

"You mean the Māori people?"

"Yes! Is that what you call them there? Go and rent it out, but I must warn you that it's not exactly a feel-good film. Did you happen to know that you live close to one of the supposedly top lodges in the world?"

No. I didn't.

Thinking about where we were living in Wairarapa, off the main tourist track with its total lack of pretense and its inherent farming simplicity, I could not imagine where this lodge might be located. "No," I answered, "I haven't heard anything about it, but I promise I'll look it up and let you know."

Soon after that conversation, I happened to be reading the Wellington *Dominion Post* and noticed that there was an advertisement for "locals" to enjoy a one-night seasonal stay for the reduced price of $999 per couple at Wharekauhau Lodge (pronounced faray-ko-ho in Māori) in the south Wairarapa, about a half-hour outside of Martinborough at Palliser Bay. Now, of course, if Carol hadn't mentioned that SHE had read about it in San Francisco, I might have just passed on this, but now I felt compelled to check it out for myself. So I rang the number and made a booking for Paul and me a few weeks later. While I was on the phone to the reception, I asked what exactly was "the deal" if the reduced price was around $1000 for a one-night stay.

"Well," the woman replied in a soft voice, "the tariff includes your luxurious accommodation, pre-dinner cocktails and canapés, a four-course gourmet dinner, cooked country breakfast and use of our indoor lap pool and gym."

"Yes," I answered, "but isn't all this included anyway with a booking?"

"Yes it is, but it is normally priced at $999 per person. This special is for a couple."

"Oh. I see."

I didn't want to turn back now, so I went ahead and gave my credit card details and hoped it would live up to its avowed claims.

And, indeed it did.

I haven't been able to justify returning to spend a night there since, given the expense and close proximity to my house. Instead, I prefer to experience this delightful property only for a long, indulgent lunch when close friends or family are visiting us. Apparently, New Zealand led the way in tourism with the concept of these luxurious all-inclusive lodges, dotted around the country on both islands. I would highly recommend anyone wanting to splurge for an important celebration or having a bit of spare change in their pockets to experience one of these properties, as they are positioned in some of the most beautiful natural settings in the country, if not the world.

To be honest, I had never heard or read anything of the Māori culture apart from seeing *The Piano* before my first visit to New Zealand in 2002, when I was first introduced to them as a people at the Living Māori Village in Rotorua. Here we paid the admission fee to get a glimpse into this native people via a walking tour around a Māori pre-fab village, complete with a formal Māori welcome, known as a pōwhiri, which involves ceremonial speeches, dances and singing before entering the marae barefoot and after the men.

My second experience was watching the national rugby team All Blacks perform a Haka dance before a tri-nations rugby game; to this day I will tune in to a game if only to see it and hear the New Zealand national anthem. I love it!

Another memorable time would have had to have been when my husband was formally welcomed to the Wairarapa District Health Board in Wairarapa by a pōwhiri and afternoon tea. This ceremony provided a rich cultural experience that I found very touching and unique to New Zealand.

No, I had never heard of the New Zealand film *Once Were Warriors* either, so decided to enquire about it at our local DVD rental store in town. After lighting the fire one chilly August evening, we all huddled around the television, knowing absolutely nothing about its storyline. After an hour or so into the film, I was intrigued by a similarity in cultures between the Māori people portrayed in the film and my own Irish culture. The singing, music, drinking and unpretentious entertaining in some of the scenes struck a familiar chord with me; some of it recalling positive warm memories of both my immediate and extended Irish family, and other not-so-pleasant memories of drunkenness, family violence and fear. Indeed, I was relieved to notice that my thirteen-year-old daughter had fallen asleep on the couch before the really disturbing scenes in the movie were played and that my son had already gone to bed, as the story line held no interest to him at all after a few minutes of watching it with us.

What an eye opener for me. Did gangs like the ones portrayed in the film really exist in New Zealand? And if so, were there any in Wairarapa? I had never heard of a gang culture being here and had I seen this film prior to moving here, I might have felt like my daughter when she saw *Whale Rider* and think to myself, Whoa! Do I really want to move there?

Throughout our years here, I have been exposed to rare gang activity, usually when members presented themselves in the E.R. after a fight. Both my husband and I noticed the similarity to L.A. gangs in their jargon and aggressive attitude, something straight out of Compton. I felt saddened that these lost souls should choose to adopt the worst of L.A. culture. If they were inclined to form a gang, why didn't they have their own culture reflected in their anti-social behavior rather than imitating a nasty American one?

* * * * *

My mother, born in Dublin, was never a big drinker. She would nurse a beer or a highball cocktail all night long. I saw her a bit giddy from alcohol only a very few times when she would join in a singsong and chat merrily with other relatives and friends. Surprisingly enough, my father did not drink when he married, but soon took to its taste once he began hanging out with other young Irish immigrants in New York at local bars for a "quick one" after work. As his drinking became more frequent and alcoholic in nature, so would his moods become more labile and tend towards abject violence and vitriolic tirades.

When viewing an iconic scene from *Once Were Warriors,* I winced with memories of my own mother being "coaxed" from her warm bed during the wee hours of the morning and ordered to cook some breakfast for some "fine lads" my father had invited back to our house after a long drinking session. The hi-fi would be turned on, and soon Irish tunes and vibrating bagpipe music would be blasting throughout the house. My poor mother had to fight off any obvious signs of resentment and fend off any unwanted drunken flirtations lest she be viewed as inhospitable to my father's new "friends." I honestly don't know how she could contain herself, but as she often told me, it was better to keep the peace rather than risk my father going off in a mad rant of verbal abuse and insults which could be triggered with as much as a perceived dirty or impatient sideways glance at him or at the scene before her.

After having lots of experiences and interactions with Māori during my time living here and working in the hospital for a few years, it has become a personal interest for me to compare the Māori to the Irish in that they both share long and tragic histories of suffering the effects of colonialism, discrimination and oppression. The Irish were the first people, I understand, to have suffered British imperialism and the Māori amongst the last. The Irish have fought the British since 1169 when Anglo-Norman troops arrived in County Wexford, whereas the Māori have in comparison a raw and fresh history with their Land Wars, a series of armed conflicts from 1845-1872 where lands were confiscated by the Crown and saw terrible and tragic events unfold in the Waikato region and the Ureweras. By the way, it is claimed that during these Land Wars, the Māori introduced the first notion of trench warfare, around the same time as the American Civil War.

Both cultures share a history of being seafaring people who love stories and embrace the oral tradition, along with being quick to grab a guitar and belt out a song with a sense of pride and passion. As the Irish are famous for their quick wit and "craic," so too are the Māori in their sense of humor and fun. Both Irish and Māori value family and extended family and are quick to welcome a stranger into their home. Even in this secular country, Māori still have lots of time to honor their dead with their culture of a wake and attendance in the local marae after a death in the family or of a friend. Similarities abound with native traditions that were molded and shaped by an ingrained pride and sense of identity with the land to which they belong. Already very much a spiritual culture like the Irish, the tendency of Māori to retain a view of myth and legend in various regions and place names with ancient stories and traditions is very comparable to the Irish tendency to do the same thing, whereas there is practically nothing evident in today's English culture of its founding roots.

Long before a written language appeared, oral traditions in both cultures enshrined the values and identity of the native people. It may be said that the essence of any cultural identity is language, and both the Irish and the Māori struggle to maintain its efficacy and practice in their own lands. This all being said, it is my belief that the Māori are more like the Irish rather than the Irish being very Māori-like, as the Irish are Europeans and had not been exposed to a Polynesian culture. In New Zealand, I feel more of an Irish sense of culture around the Māori people and gatherings than I feel around the European descendants, most of whom herald from English and Scottish settlers and some seem lacking in an unreserved sense of genuine warmth, fun, reckless abandonment and generosity when welcoming a stranger into their circles.

Whereas the Irish have always maintained a very strong sense of identity and culture throughout centuries of occupation, the Māori continue to struggle to define their place in present-day New Zealand society with a sense of satisfaction and pride.

Morning Tea, Smokos and California Dreamin'

WHAT A LOVELY CUSTOM: MORNING Tea. I suppose we would have simply called it taking a work break back in California, but here it is viewed not only as a work break, but rather an important social custom imported from the British. It is a time of the morning, usually around 10:30 or so, put aside for a cuppa, a bikkie, or if one preferred, a smoko, to use colloquial language. These breaks are written as such into work contracts as well, stating a ten-minute period is put aside for morning and afternoon tea. Very often, a work morning is scheduled around this precious time, morning tea. Meetings in town are arranged around it as well, with café tables filling rapidly from around 10:30 a.m. onwards to lunch.

The thing I like most about meeting someone for morning tea in town, rather than lunch, is that it's a rather open-ended engagement in terms of how long it's expected to last. So, if one just wanted a quick cup of tea or coffee and then had to run off, it would not be considered rude. On the other hand, if there was no pressing engagement until lunchtime, the time taken for morning tea could well extend into an hour. Smokos are viewed just as important a work break in the day for those in need of a nicotine fix, to have a chit-chat and a cigarette to escape the workplace for a short spell in the morning and afternoon.

After a few weeks here, I was invited by one of the local doctors' wives, Taoni, who had a daughter in Catherine's year, to join her and her former "play-group" for morning tea. She didn't want to hear my excuses about not being the type of person who ever did the "meet for coffee" thing back in the USA. She was originally from South Africa, and at that time most of the medical staff in the hospital hailed from South Africa. I was taxed to find some genuine Kiwis. "You must come along," she commanded me. "The women in this group are all Kiwis, and they will help you a great deal by giving you their input on local things like where to buy the best meat, how to find a decent handymen and other essential general insider knowledge. They're a great group of women."

So, I decided to give it a go. She was quite insistent on picking me up after doing her usual early morning eight kilometer jog (she's a fitness freak) around the lovely swan-laden Henley Lake in town and taking me to the house where it was to be hosted that week.

The women in the group had forged a long history together throughout the years, with their kids going through the same school system and sport activities; as such, I felt very much an outsider at that first gathering. I sat quietly and sipped my tea, not wanting to be the loud, know-it-all American. After a very self-conscious half-hour or so, I was finally acknowledged and asked how I was "finding it" in Wairarapa. I responded all smiles and said it was wonderful indeed to be in such a lovely town. They all looked at me incredulously, then at one another, shaking their heads.

"Surely this must be quite different from what you left behind in San Diego?" I was asked.

Yes, I assured them, it was vastly different, and that's precisely why we decided to move to this country. I tried to explain as briefly as possible that it was the high quality of lifestyle, with no abject poverty, slums, pollution, cramped city living, major health care issues and traffic that was the drawing card for us. That the North and the South Islands combined are roughly the same land size as Colorado, Japan or the UK, and being populated with slightly over four million people—that's roughly thirty-three million less than the state of California—affords easy escape from the crowds and all the problems that occur with urban densely populated areas.

What I really needed to learn from this group was where could I leave my husband's shirts to be done, as in laundered and pressed, and a recommendation for an experienced housekeeper.

"What do you mean, have your husband's shirts *done?*" one woman asked me after an uncomfortable pause in the conversation.

"You know, a dry cleaner that washes and irons shirts," I answered matter-of-factly.

"What? You're saying you can't launder and iron them yourself?"

I sank deeper into my seat and grabbed my cup of coffee.

Well, dropping shirts off at the local cleaners is simply not done in these parts. It would be considered a costly and wasteful extravagance. And housekeepers? "What's a housekeeper?" they asked. "Oh . . . you mean a cleaner, don't you?"

They looked at me once again with a surprised air about them. Again, not really the "done" thing here; whereas from where I had just moved, it would be considered out of the norm NOT to have a housekeeper. Well, truly I was not in Encinitas anymore. I hadn't scrubbed a toilet or ironed a shirt in years, and now I was going to have to start? Undeterred, I called into a local dry cleaner on the way home and asked about laundering and ironing men's shirts.

"You mean just regular men's work shirts?" I was asked.

"Well," I tried to explain, "my husband wears a shirt and tie to work every day, and usually a different one every day as well."

"Oh, so your husband must be the new surgeon at the hospital, then," the lady behind the counter said, smiling. "I see. Well, it usually costs about $5.50 per shirt." she said with some hesitation. "Of course, if you bring in more than five at a time, we could give you a deal."

I was stunned. $5.50 per shirt? I was paying no more than a dollar back in San Diego. I decided I would try to save the $100 or so a month at the dry cleaners and do what everyone else in town did; that is, do it myself, in the true DIY mentality that characterizes Kiwis. But after about two months, I became quickly overwhelmed with mounds of shirts waiting to be ironed and eventually caved in and brought the next load of dirty ones to the same dry cleaners. I was promised a fifty-cent per shirt discount, which sounded fair enough to me. Now, I know that many American women don't iron but an Irish-born mother, who was never fond of clothes dryers and therefore ironed many things, including sheets and jeans, raised me. I tried to practice a middle ground where ironing was concerned, and restricted my own personal items to pillowcases, cloth napkins, and my own trousers and shirts. I was telling this to another recent American immigrant, a quite outspoken and rather opinionated woman who gave me a look that made me feel I was some pathetic, wasteful human being, not appreciative of God's greatest gift: time.

"What are you going to say," she demanded, "in your defense at the Pearly Gates when St. Peter looks at you? 'Susan!' he's going to say. 'You were given X many hours on earth, and you spent how many of these ironing?'"

Ummm . . . .

After some careful consideration, I didn't fully agree with her implication that I was wasting precious time ironing. It gives me a certain joy and pride to place an ironed pillowcase on my pillow and to pull out ironed cloth napkins when dining formally.

So, the time of reckoning was upon me: no housekeepers and no real affordable laundering service in my newly adopted land. Nor morning beach walks with my friends or sunset margaritas with complimentary salsa and chips at one of the many beachfront cafés near my house. No excitement at the prospect of seeing a sunset "green flash" at said beachfront café. No more deliveries of my favorite local magazines, *Sunset, Gourmet, Saveur* or *Bon Appétit*. And warm, sunny weather seemed to be a distant memory as it teemed rain almost every day since we'd arrived in Wairarapa. I hadn't swum or aqua-jogged in weeks.

The September school holidays were upon us after only a few weeks of arriving to Wairarapa and we decided to do a road trip up the east coast to Gisborne, where Alex had a friend living that boarded at his school. On our first trip back in 2002, we had driven down the center of the North Island from Auckland, as most tourists do their first time to New Zealand and missed the sights on both coasts. We had seen a picture book of Gisborne back in San Diego before we moved as one of our neighbors happened to surf every morning with a Kiwi guy from that area. It looked to be a laid-back beach town drenched in sunshine and we were excited to visit there.

We broke up the drive and stayed a night in the Hawkes Bay in the cute little sophisticated town, Havelock North. While there, we went to the Sunday farmer's market nearby in Hastings and immediately felt a longing for our California lives as we viewed and tasted all the fresh produce and goods being sold there. The area was buzzing with live music, the grinding of coffee beans and the enticing smell of sausages on the grill. Catherine was quick to wonder why we hadn't moved there instead of Wairarapa.

The road to Gisborne from Hawkes Bay requires the driver's full concentration and attention, as it is very narrow, winding and busy with large logging trucks and stray goats. I thought it went on and on for ages and was well over it by the time we drove into the center of Gisborne, with its streets lined with palm trees and tables filled with folk sipping coffee outside cozy little cafés. It held an immediate appeal for me. A few kilometers outside Gisborne is Wainui Beach, where Alex's friend lived, which is a very popular surfing spot well known throughout the country. I had booked us into a motel a block from the beach; within minutes, the surfboard was being lifted from the car with Alex heading straight for the waves.

Everyone was happy and excited to see the expansive ocean and empty beach. While Alex hit the surf, the rest of us walked along the beach, enjoying the views to the distant headlands. After three days there, we still were not ready to leave, but had plans to visit friends in Auckland. So, with promises to return, we got back on the road. A few years later, we actually bought a little house there and continue to enjoy the area and build memories with the wonderful local friends from all over the world we've been lucky to meet. The relative isolation of the area and its many beaches along the East Cape is magic.

Shortly after returning home from that road trip, I ached and had strong longings for all the things in my past life I'd previously taken advantage of. I was missing my friends and our social life very much. As I'd been driving Alex to school that morning, my quiet preoccupation must have alarmed him; he looked over and delicately asked me if everything was OK.

Immediately, I tried—probably with a tad too much enthusiasm—to assure him all was great, but he turned to me and said very calmly, "You know, Mom, you can't let yourself get down. We're all doing well here because of you. If you go to the dark side, we'll all crumble. This whole move will fall apart. You've got to get back to your old self."

Oh . . . from the mouth of babes.

Whoa! Well . . . thanks for that, Alex. No pressure at all. The thought of faking cheerfulness and positivity was enough in itself to make me more depressed. Couldn't I be permitted to wallow once in a while in my perceived misery and loneliness? Apparently not, as my family depended on me to be their anchor. In that regard, it was just as well I was not working and free to support any situation or emotion when called upon. Yes, there were definitely times when I wondered, Oh my God, what the hell have we done?

Fortunately these doubts would not linger long, as I stared at the distant hills, took a deep breath of very fresh air, and watched the river in flood from my window thundering over boulders and rocks under the bridge at the north end of town. I would again be struck with the untamed beauty and wildness of it all. The space. The light. The scraggly, barren vines waiting to come alive in a few weeks' time with fresh, green grape leaves. It was all-good. Opening a bottle of local pinot noir from Martinborough while cooking dinner helped the mood as well, and all would seem right with the world.

At least for a few hours.

Docking Ships to Docking Lambs

A FEW MONTHS AFTER WE HAD moved, Alex came home excited about the prospect of taking a job over the upcoming school holidays; docking lambs on a friend's farm located about twenty minutes' further east from us in the country. Now, what the heck is docking? I soon learned that it involves removing most of the lamb's tail to prevent the build-up of dags on the wool around the sheep's rear end, or bum. Excrement tends to collect around the sheep's bum, and form crusty, poopy dags. These dags attract blowflies, which strike and then the sheep becomes "blown." Soon the fly's maggots eat the sheep's flesh and cause great distress. Docking is meant to avoid this distress, and is best done around six weeks of age with the use of rubber rings.

Now I am describing a scene here which involves a San Diego coastal surfer boy who is going on and on with such passion about docking lambs. He left a city where docking referred only to local cruise ships arriving in port or Navy ships out on exercises. So, Alex rises early, excited as can be while he packs a lunch, and he is collected in a farm ute outside our front door at a chilly 6:00 a.m. one morning and driven up to a nearby farm. There he helps guide the lambs into fenced-off areas, and proceeds to hold them down to be docked. He described the screeches of the ewes and the bleating of the lambs as deafening once they were separated from one another so the work could begin. How they were all reunited with one another by the end of the day still remains a mystery to him.

Let it be known that Alex is a hard worker when he sets to task and it annoyed him increasingly and to no end when the call for a "smoko" came just as they were making serious headway into docking. He would have preferred to just have kept at it, and then knock off work a bit earlier than planned. But he isn't addicted to nicotine, so would have no understanding or patience for stopping the flow of work to engage in such an unhealthy act. He was indeed shocked to learn that men were as capable of sharing juicy gossip, similar to a group of idle women, as he listened to the farmers exchanging updates and tidbits about neighbors and friends.

After three full days of this, he relayed to his friend's father that he would not be available to work the last day, as we were all taking off on a road-trip up to the East Cape. Seeing the men's disappointed faces, he advised them nonchalantly that they might find some day laborers to take his place. Now this suggestion really brought on some confused stares.

"What do you mean by day laborers?" one of the men asked.

"Ah, you know . . . ," said Alex, "aren't there some local guys standing on corners that might be looking for a day job?"

Well, the men apparently just roared laughing.

"Yeah right, mate!! More like standing on the corner waiting for the benefit," one replied.

Man oh man . . . talk about a cultural divide. And total ignorance of this native New Zealand culture.

So Alex was to quickly learn that this was NOT the norm here in Wairarapa as it was in Encinitas, San Diego. Many a morning on the way to school, he would witness hopeful-looking Mexican men standing patiently on street corners, holding their lunch boxes and eagerly waiting to get picked up for day work as a laborer in the fields or on a building site, and expecting to be paid minimum wages in cash for their efforts. Meanwhile, their wives worked in many of the local houses cleaning, doing laundry and minding young children to put food in the mouths of their own family.

Of course it would not be the same here, as New Zealand does not have any idea what it's like to have an illegal immigrant population. The Statue of Liberty remains an American icon of freedom and a welcoming sight to immigrants arriving from abroad, but often immigration services cannot keep up with the influx of those seeking a better life and the dream of prosperity, especially those coming illegally across the border from Mexico every day. It is a complicated economic and political situation, and one that I was happy to leave behind in California. I was happy to no longer listen and forcefully bite my tongue to all the incessant complaining and whingeing of friends about the illegal alien problem while many of them employed such folk to raise their children, clean their houses, tend to their gardens, wash their cars and scrub their boats and then pay them cash with no regard to taxes being paid, health insurance or workman's compensation for these people. This was a life I left behind.

But back to the sheep and iconic Kiwi activities . . . .

Wairarapa's claim to fame is hosting the world-renowned Golden Shears competition every year and Paul and I were fortunate to get an invitation from one of the organizers to join their private table on the opening night. And what an event it is! The speed with which these sheep were shorn by both electric shears and hand-held shears was beyond belief.

In the atmosphere of a real country hoe-down, minus all the cowboy hats, I sat and watched brawny men clad in singlets and shorts drape themselves over sheep and work on them for what seemed liked seconds before all their wool lay at their feet on the floor. I really felt as if I were in a scene from the film *The Thornbirds*. Prizes were awarded for many categories, including the fastest, the most precise and one for women judged for wool sorting. In fact, there recently an article on this event in the *Wall Street Journal* my friend in California enthusiastically shared with me.

While at the Golden Shears, Paul and I were invited to meet some friends the next day about a half-hour outside town to watch the Sheep Dog Trials, another activity I had never heard of in my life and had no clue to what it entailed. So, we figured, what the heck, let's go. We threw some Wellington boots (gum boots as they are called here) and a couple of walking sticks into the boot of the car and off we drove east from Wairarapa, keeping our eyes open for a sign indicating the event. We were directed into a paddock filled with parked cars and watched men walk by, clad in oilskin western-styled hats, long coats, gum boots and clasping walking sticks as their working dogs ambled obediently about them. Our friends called over to us and we were soon learning the history and rules of this sport, which is well founded in New Zealand, over 125 years old at that.

The first trial we watched featured driver dogs. These dogs were let off by their owner at the bottom of the field, and instructed by loud verbal commands and whistles to head up the hill to a tight cluster of sheep that had just been guided to a designated spot by another dog, called the liberator. We watched in fascination as the driver dog scampered effortlessly up the steep hill to arrive just above the flock of sheep, and stay put for a few minutes. This is called The Introduction of the Dog. There the dog remains and begins to stare down the sheep, in an effort to let them know who's the boss. Obeying the commands of its owner standing below at the bottom of the hill, the dog creeps ever so slowly and patiently towards the sheep. The dog must assert its authority at this stage, otherwise the sheep will lose all respect and fear and go on about their business, which is simply grazing. Points are taken away from the owner if the dog barks, or the sheep start running willy-nilly in all directions. The goal of this exercise is for the dog to stare down the sheep quietly and direct them down the hill in an orderly stroll to an obstacle course down below and into a designated holding pen. Truly captivating stuff.

Next, we viewed the huntaway dog trials. These New Zealand-bred dogs use their barking and force of presence to herd sheep up the hill within a well-defined course marked out by the event organizers. Standing there mingling with the farmers and local spectators in the soft sporadic rain filled me with a sense of surrealism. I stared around me at the rolling dark lush landscape dotted with sheep and working dogs, thinking, *Wow!* I'm definitely not in San Diego anymore.

Twelve years on down the road, I often wonder if I am really any better off by having moved from my idyllic spot in the world. And, if I am better off, in what ways? I can't see anything better when I look in the mirror, and though I feel it is healthier here not to be obsessed with plastic surgery or weight, I can't help but feel a bit frumpy when I return to visit my old friends in California. They all look so fabulous, and then I must remind myself that it is Southern California after all, the land of perfect teeth and enhanced bodies.

In the first few weeks after moving here, I went to see a dentist in Wellington, having chipped two veneers upon chomping down impatiently on a gingernut biscuit before bed one night. After his examination, he quickly remarked that I had a real "California mouth," what with my crowns and veneers. It happened to be a very expensive gingernut biscuit and when I was painfully paying the couple of thousand dollars for the repair, the receptionist looked up at me and whispered, "You know, you're meant to dip the biscuits into your tea."

I smiled at her and shared, "I know. I was just being a bit greedy is all. I won't do that again!"

No doubt about it, I was indeed a very privileged Californian in my day. But the greatest sense of privilege has been felt because we moved and started a new life in a new country. It's a greater sense of living life as an adventure. In fact, I often still find myself staring in awe out the windows of my house looking west to the mountains and am filled with nothing but gratitude and appreciation for this spectacular view, this privileged life I am living.

Kiwi Identity

W HEN I FIRST MOVED HERE, I would ask out of curiosity from where someone's family originated and was always met with an air of puzzlement. *What do you mean "where am I from?" I'm a Kiwi.*

Yes, I would continue, but where is your family from? What is your heritage? This is a colonized country after all.

It was the rare person who answered me with certainty and a sense of pride that their ancestors hailed from England, or Scotland or Ireland, the UK in general, or elsewhere in Europe, especially from the Netherlands. The fierce need to distance themselves from their familial cultural heritage and forge a totally new identity, as "Kiwi" impressed me profoundly. I reminded myself that New Zealand was such a young country in comparison to the United States, lagging behind about 200 years in colonization, and the descendants of the original founders were adamant about establishing a different and unique culture by cutting off all ties to the Mother Country.

Only when really pressed by me, would I hear that their grandmother, or some not-too-distant relative was from England, or Ireland, etcetera, but that was all that was forthcoming. There was no sense of allegiance to their heritage, as one finds in the United States. When an American is asked on American soil from what nationality one heralds, the answer would rarely be "I'm an American." One would preface it with a cultural background or indeed many cultural backgrounds. I've listened many times to some folk describe in great detail their ethnic background in percentages . . . as in 10% English, 25% French, etc.

It was not long that I was introduced to the term Pākehā, a term reserved for those of European-New Zealand descent. This identity was forged as a result of the pioneering and rural history of New Zealand, about the time of the Land Wars of 1860s, when the native Māori suffered a loss of land and identity. New Zealand was largely felt to be a "classless" society until recently, with one's station resting with culture: one was either Pākehā, or Māori. The term Pākehā is still very much in use, and I wonder with what generation is the label deemed no longer relevant? With globalization, New Zealand is indeed becoming a multi-cultural lot, with Auckland claiming to be the largest Polynesian city in the world. Most are presently content to say they are New Zealanders or Kiwis, rather than use the term Pākehā. Indeed, the last time I was visiting friends in Auckland and walked down Queen Street, I truly did not feel that I was in New Zealand as there was such a predominance of Asian people everywhere, who would probably identify themselves as Kiwis.

God forbid though, if you mistook a Kiwi for an Australian. In my early days trying to assimilate here, I made a conscious effort to downplay the very apparent fact that I was American, as the Iraqi war was in full swing, and the fiercely unpopular George W. Bush was up for re-election that first November 2004 after we had moved here. His name was on the tip of everyone's tongue in almost every conversation. He was vehemently despised. This imparted a very distinct anti-American sentiment in the air, which often left me feeling quite uncomfortable and defensive. I cringed when one would start a conversation with "Well, the Americans do this, or believe this . . . ," or to me personally, "You Americans think . . . ."

Sometimes my husband responded, "What Americans do you mean? Those who live in Maine, Texas, Iowa, New York, California . . . ?"

You see, we are a huge, multi-cultural bunch and live over a vast and diverse land. We cannot be clumped together in a blanket statement such as *You Americans*.

It was only after moving to New Zealand that I learned what a major role the Americans played in World War II, protecting and defending Australia's and New Zealand's borders from Japanese invasion—and I have a degree in U.S. History from San Francisco State University. As England had most of its armed forces bogged down in Europe, President Roosevelt promised Winston Churchill with a commitment to freedom and democracy that the United States would protect Allied countries after the fall of Singapore.

One fine day shortly after moving here, I was walking along the beautiful Wellington harbor waterfront and noticed a commemorative plaque thanking all the Americans who landed there (to great fanfare and welcome) on 14 June 1942. Between 1942 and 1944, over 15,000 American soldiers lived in Wellington alone. My older neighbor in Wellington told me how grateful they were to see all the Yanks arriving in Wellington Harbor as they were terrified of the Japanese, who had just bombed their friends across the ditch in Darwin. They felt their prayers had been answered. My New Zealand peers, however, born in the baby boom generation, don't seem to share this sense of gratitude for the American "invasion" as did their parents who are now in their late eighties. Indeed, when I mentioned this to someone in the morning tea group, a woman responded with a smirk, "Oh yes, the Yanks were here all right. What was it they said about them? Over-paid, over-sexed and over-here."

The Brits supposedly said the same thing, until an American officer taunted back, "Well, you lot are under-paid, under-fed, under-sexed and under Eisenhower!"

A more extreme expression of the anti-American sentiment of that time was to be experienced at a local school during a sermon given, no less, by a female chaplain addressing a small group of Japanese exchange students. Our friend's son relayed to us over dinner one evening how he cringed when the chaplain apologized to the young Japanese exchange students sitting before her for the horrors and suffering inflicted upon them by the Americans who dropped the atomic bombs to end the war. She apparently was not aware there was an American student in the chapel who was thinking, Hey wait a minute! Doesn't anybody here remember Pearl Harbor?

I really should have made a formal complaint to the headmaster, but then again I did not want to draw attention to us as the "ugly Americans" and have our son potentially chastised for this at school. But it is in this manner younger generations learn to form negative opinions of other nations, which often rise from ignorance, prejudice and jealousy.

Soon after this incident, Paul had his usual calm composure tested by a junior doctor while making morning rounds at the hospital. This person apparently had some issues and perhaps a cultural chip on her shoulder as well. She forcefully imposed her views and would make inappropriate and disparaging comments during the morning surgical rounds about American politics, American culture and occasionally, American medicine, which my husband would usually dismiss with a shrug and just let it go.

In the United States, junior doctors would never address a consultant in such a casual and informal manner while on hospital rounds. This one day she felt the need once again to assert herself and her identity as a peace-loving Kiwi, citing New Zealand's stand on nuclear warships, when my husband turned to her and asked: "Tell me, what do you think would happen if New Zealand were to be suddenly sucked into the Pacific Ocean and completely vanished from the planet? Do you think the world would suddenly stand still? And if so, for how long? Would all trade stop? Would Wall Street shut down and all business come to an end? And would human civilization, as we know it, suddenly cease to be? Please. Just do me a big favor and get over yourself."

There were no further comments from this particular person again.

In that vein, after President Obama was elected in 2008, my confidence grew immeasurably as an American living in New Zealand. At the end of the day, it was all part of the teething pains we endured as we grew accustomed to the culture of our newly adopted country. New Zealand is now what I call home and I find it still a very delightful and enviable place to live. I now feel more settled in my place here, as I am a New Zealand citizen and now hold a New Zealand passport.

I can also have a bit of fun as in at lunch recently with some friends in Wellington when the discussion turned to American health care. One of the ladies at the table turned to me and said, "It's no wonder *your* healthcare system in America is a mess. *You* put all your money into the military and fighting wars."

Placed uncomfortably on the defensive, I calmly answered, "Yes, that's right. Keeping you lot all safe down here at the bottom of the world."

I sensed this comment took her completely off guard, as she fidgeted a bit before saying, "Well, I don't entirely believe all that."

I remained unapologetic for my remark, feeling that if someone can dish it out to me they need to be able to take it back.

It is my thought that there would be considerably less angst amongst New Zealanders if they were to accept the fact that they are not likely destined to be a serious world player with regards to military strength or natural resources purely because of the size of the country. And take a deep breath and applaud what they do have: stunning scenery, clean air, fantastic lifestyle and a hard-working, DIY, generous attitude, topped off with a wicked sense of humor.

My sense of gratitude increases as time goes on and truly alarming events unfold every day in other parts of the world.

This is truly my little slice of heaven.

Sweet As

THE FIRST MONTH SAW ME taking care of necessary housekeeping chores, such as opening a local bank account and applying for a credit card and an ATM card, while keeping a constant eye on the currency exchange rate to know when to wire over our precious American dollars. After I had finished with the lovely, unhurried local bank manager, she smiled and told me everything was "good as gold" and I was handed a large folder in which I was instructed to keep "all my bits and pieces." Lovely!

As we had only one car, I was the chauffeur for the first few months. After dropping my husband off at the hospital down the road and taking the children to their schools, I would usually set out on foot to explore the town, and pick up something for dinner along the way. My first mission was to source some fresh jumbo prawns, so we may "throw them on the barbie" at our home in New Zealand as we had done in Sydney. I had noticed several shops in town called "Fish Supply," so naturally I figured this is where fresh fish could be purchased. One morning when I sauntered around the corner to the local fish supply shop, I was met with a puzzled look and an apology when I asked for jumbo prawns. Undaunted, I decided to try some of the other fish supply shops in town. While enroute, I passed a shop advertising "Sammies." Having no idea what that might be, I walked into the café-style eatery and asked, "Excuse me. Could you please tell me what a 'sammie' is?"

Again, I was given the same puzzled look with which the person in the fish shop had responded, and then was told, quite matter-of-factly, "You know? Sammies."

"Uh, no. I actually don't know," I assured her with a smile. I imagined she was going to ask me next from which planet did I come, but instead she offered, "You know, the things you fold over to put meat or cheese in between, and heat up, like "toasties".

"Oh. OK," I answered, now doubly confused, wondering what a toastie might be and how it related to a sammie.

I continued to stare at her vacantly when it dawned on me that this was a lunch place and she was probably referring to a New Zealand version of a sandwich bar. Feeling like a total idiot, I thanked her and walked out of the shop and back on my original quest to find fresh jumbo prawns. It was only at the third fish supply store where I was given an explanation that would arrest any further attempts or hopes of emulating the Sydney-type "barbie" experience.

"No, afraid no fresh prawns here in New Zealand. Our waters are way too cold, not like the Aussie seas. You might want to give Moore-Wilson's a try and see what they have in the freezer. Good as gold," smiled the gentleman dressed in a white long butcher's coat and white knee-high rubber boots.

"I'm sorry, Moore what?" I asked, wondering what the heck that might be, and if it was within walking distance.

I was directed down the street to a large warehouse-type building, which sold an expansive array of high quality meats, varied Asian foodstuffs, fresh produce, and boasted aisles and aisles of imported canned and bottled products. It reminded me of a very dressed-down cross between the Trader Joe's and Costco stores back in San Diego. I walked over to the fresh produce area and stared at fruit I had not heard of before, such as tamarillos and feijoas. Bell peppers were labeled capsicums and Swiss chard was called silver beet. Suddenly, I had an ache in my heart for what I'd left behind in my former stores: the variety, the year-round fresh fruit, the abundance, including fresh jumbo prawns, anytime or any season I wanted them. And what about Alaskan king crab legs? Would I ever see them again?

I found the deep freeze section of Moore-Wilson's and began scanning the rows for prawns; soon I was rewarded to find boxes of them, with their heads still intact, frozen rock hard and imported from: Thailand! All good. I would simply defrost them and make do. After all, they could be barbecued as easily as fresh ones and would probably taste as good. Since that mission, I have spotted on rare occasions the jumbo banana prawns from Australia on sale at a few select markets in Wellington and up in sunny Gisborne, and at least a dozen or so of them make it into my shopping cart and are soon tossed on the barbie and washed down with a cheeky little chilled New Zealand "sauvy."

Indeed, I've no doubts that in those early days of settling in I may have been perceived as being a tad slow on the uptake, as I honestly could not understand what was being communicated to me in the New Zealand accent. Aside from getting used to local idioms and the patterns of speech, I had to remind myself that this was indeed the English language being spoken in this part of the world and not some foreign dialect. When one of the neighbors asked me why the children were not taking the bus to school, I told them I didn't know where it stopped. She informed me it was just across the street from the dairy.

"Yes, but where is that place, the dairy?" I asked her, imagining I would be driving out of town a bit, and dropping the kids off by rows of cows waiting to be milked every morning. She stared a moment. "The dairy? Why, it's on the corner down the street from you."

"Oh!" I answered. "You mean the little market, the Tip-Top?"

Once again, I was given "the look." After a few awkward moments, I deciphered that the corner market was not called the "Tip-Top," which was in fact the name of an ice creamery served within and that paid to have its name advertised all over the outside. Oh! And the dairy . . . ? This is the name given to these local neighborhood convenience markets, as they originally opened to sell things like milk, eggs, and other basic staples, rather like a 7/11 store. OK, thanks. Got it.

After a time, in an effort not to ask the speaker to kindly repeat several times over what the heck he or she was saying before I understood, I decided it was more useful for me to have certain words I had missed simply spelled out. For this purpose, a writing pad was duly purchased and kept in my handbag. Thus it was during my first few weeks exploring Wellington, I was asking a random person for directions to a sushi restaurant in town and as the young fellow garbled on and on quickly, I strained to catch only the bits where he said, " . . . Well, go there and make a right"

"I'm sorry. Go where?" I asked, hoping he would speak a bit slower.

Again, I received "the look." "Uh, you know Manna Maw, right?" he asked with a certainty that rendered me even more pathetic.

"Manna Maw? No, I'm afraid I don't. Uh, is it around here?"

"Manna Maw?"

It was clearly time for further elucidation in the way of the written word.

"Would you mind doing me a huge favor?" I asked, as I reached into my handbag for a pen and my new notepad. "Would you please spell that for me?"

"No worries," he answered, displaying polite patience as he began slowly spelling M A N N E R S   M A L L."

"Oh! Manners Mall. Now I get it. OK. So I go to Manners Mall, and . . . ?"

In my personal experience, New Zealanders, for the most part, do not pronounce their R's, or L's at the end of a word, and do not use the short "E" vowel sound in their diction, to name but a few peculiarities. So, egg is pronounced eeeeg, and leg, leeeeg, and so on. A double-L at the end of a word becomes a W, thus Mall becomes Maw, and G in the middle of a word is usually silent. The city of Melbourne, which we as Americans were pronouncing Mel-Borne, is pronounced here as Mel-Bun.

It was also very frustrating for both Paul and I to try and decipher voice messages on our cell phones and home answering machine. I'd have to replay each word individually over and over a few times, and then write down what I thought the words were until I understood it. And I could not for the life of me tell the difference between a Kiwi, a South African, English or an Australian accent for that matter. Indeed, I have come a long way in my time here, now possessing quite a discerning ear for the varied colonists' tongue.

The frosty mornings were soon giving way to warmer days with blossoms appearing on the trees and glad tidings of spring in the air. It proved entertaining in those early days to hear the children recount tales from their daily school experiences. Catherine entertained us frequently with some of the more salient messages from the weekly assemblies at school. She was getting the accent down very well by this stage.

"Gulls! (Girls) Gulls . . . do listen up," Catherine began, imitating the vice principal's address at assembly that morning around the dinner table one night. "Gulls! . . . It has come to my attention that some of you are wearing dark undergarments which can be seen through your school blouse. This is not a good look. Please restrict yourselves to either white or beige undergarments from here on out."

Kenmare College, where Alex was a day student in his next-to-last year, sported an air of decorum and discipline which belied its daily *Lost Boys* activities. Its tranquil park-like grounds were complete with a defunct golf course and a winding river running behind the campus on the southern outskirts of town.

Alex, being a keen fly-fisherman, took to exploring the river every chance he could in between classes and on his lunch hour. Noticing that he kept disappearing into the "bush," one of the boys came up to him and remarked, "Good on ya, mate! You're here only a few days and you've already sussed out where all the smokos hang."

Being a vehement anti-smoker, Alex assured him he was instead looking for trout, and surprised everyone the next day when he showed up to school with his fishing pole and tackle box. Aside from smoking, none of the other boys went down to the river—outside of summer to take a dip—and so, after watching with interest this perceived cool Californian dude fishing unapologetically, it was only a matter of time before a few other fishermen "came out of the closet" and joined him after school.

Noticing the swift current in the river, Alex thought of another seasonal activity and carried his surfboard to school one day. Boys stared in bewilderment wondering what he intended to do with a surfboard on campus as the beach was an hour away. It was stored in the cloakroom until after school, when he donned a wetsuit and jumped into the river and began padding forcefully against the current. "I want to build up my upper body strength" was the reason given to the curious bystanders. He was clearly missing the morning and evening workout he had been used to with his surf P.E. class back in San Diego.

More eyebrows were raised in those first months when he asked one of his buddies where he could buy some bird seed in town to fill the empty feeders we had brought along with us from San Diego.

"Bird feeders?" one of the boys quipped. "What the hell would you buy bird seed for, eh? Plant a tree, mate!" A no brainer.

And soon our bird feeders were sadly made redundant.

Tongues wagged wildly at this American boy's rather ordinary past-times, as his peers were expecting afternoons of wild partying as viewed on television where beer and alcohol was sipped from large red plastic cups, those purchased in bulk from Costco. "They think it's a real American thing to drink from those red cups, Mom." He told me one day. "Can I bring some to school?"

After a month or so, I wondered why there were no school friends stopping by for a visit or a sleepover, as was always the case back home. Seemingly, the boys and girls in the area had been weaned from childhood to young adulthood on such American sitcoms as *Orange County* and thus had certain expectations from their new American classmates. To their disappointment, my children did not drink, or smoke pot, or hold wild parties at their parent's house at weekends, or have multiple sexual dramas, at least not at that stage of their lives. Sadly, I learned these unrealistic expectations intimidated our children and prevented them from inviting friends home lest they disappoint and be viewed as ordinary as everyone else around them.

Occasionally Alex received invitations from some of the weekly boarders who lived in the country to spend the weekend at their home and was rewarded with some unique experiences. To be honest, I wish I had been spared some of the shocking details at the time, such as the rather cavalier approach to hunting and the possession and safe use of firearms.

Alex had been away for one weekend with one of the boarders who lived on a huge dairy farm in the wild southern Wairarapa coast. He called me on a Sunday afternoon on his cell phone once he came back into satellite coverage to ask if he may spend the night at the boarding house at school, as they were running late and his friend had to sign in by early evening for compulsory Chapel service. And so I gave him permission without too much thought.

As the boys were running late, they drove straight to the campus for fear of getting a "tardy" card, which had Hamish more concerned than the fact the pair of them were returning to school in their hunting gear. Once the Chapel service was over, they returned to the junior boarding house, and to the marvel of the young boys, skillfully plucked the feathers and dressed the ducks and carefully lifted off the breast with a pocketknife, which seemingly every boy owned and carried on their person.

The duck breast was then placed on an electric panini sandwich grill (very resourceful, I thought) and served up perfectly cooked in five minutes or so. Some orange marmalade jam was quickly heated in the microwave and poured over the warm breast and a small taste of duck a l'orange was served to all the boys as part of their evening tea. After the day's shooting was discussed at length in the boarding house, the junior boys promptly cleared the mess and lights put out for the night.

The next day, he came home still buzzing from all the weekend's activities. "I had such a fun time," he began. "Hamish and I went duck shooting and nabbed two, then brought them back to the junior house and cooked them up for the boys."

Duck shooting? What? How did he do that?

With shotguns, I was quickly told. Real guns.

Oh? "And what did you do with the guns?" I asked.

"Oh, his father took them back home with him. But Hamish told me that once, a while back when he was at school in the South Island, he had to bring his gun to school with the ammunition and all as he didn't have time to drop it off home."

"What?"

"Yeah, and the headmaster was cool with that as long as he had it locked up in his wardrobe."

I could not believe what I was hearing. Where else could this very scene have taken place?

Well, my imagination went wild in a few seconds in an attempt to imagine this happening back at his old school in San Diego. A SWAT team would have surely surrounded the school and the premises put on lock-down within minutes of learning there was a gun locked away somewhere on the campus. It would have been instant news on all the major TV stations. How refreshing it was not to have this same mentality—or whatever it is in the U.S. that makes them so dangerously gun happy—in New Zealand.

I soon learned that once school lessons had finished for the day, the day pupils would queue up for the bus while their boarder classmates would race to their rooms, strip off the regulation uniform and run barefoot and shirtless with their pocket knives in hand to build forts in the nearby bush. The apparent strict code of behavior masked the uncensored freedom they enjoyed after class, which is not to be had any longer in the U.S., what with the constant threat of being sued, school shootings and the more recent fears of terrorism. How could I have been surprised then when Alex asked me if he could be part of this *Lost Boys* world and become a weekly boarder for his last year? He wanted the camaraderie, the sense of fraternity and belonging to the special club he perceived only the boarders enjoyed, even though we lived only a ten-minute drive away from the campus. It was to become a unique cherished memory from our early days here.

Southerlies and Skirt Steak

AS OFTEN HAPPENS WITH HAVING school-aged children, I was introduced and became friends by default with some of the parents of my children's friends. Aengus, whose grandmother happened to live next door to our rental in town, was one of Alex's first friends. Like Alex, Aengus was a keen surfer and soon invited him to catch some waves over a weekend at their other property out on the coast, which I later learned was an 8,600-acre sheep station with hills filled with wild deer and pigs and which included ten kilometers of prime coastline, teeming with abalone (paua) and Pacific lobsters (crayfish). Truly, a bloke's *Heaven-Haven*.

One Friday afternoon, Aengus' father, Jonathan, appeared at our back door donning jeans, a black merino wool jersey and an oil-skinned western hat; the epitome of the ruggedly handsome, iconic New Zealand bush fellow. Extremely pleasant and excited to have Alex along for the weekend, he advised him to bring along some rain gear and warm clothes.

"There's a fierce Southerly meant to be blowing through this evening. And there's nothing between Antarctica and New Zealand to slow it down. So, best to rug-up," he smiled around at us.

"A Southerly?" I asked, not knowing the implications of this unfriendly wind until I felt the effects of it one afternoon in Wellington. A rather pleasant winter day turned angry when the temperature rapidly plummeted ten degrees Celsius as the Southerly hit the city with its sheets of freezing gusts and horizontal rain. It blasts its way up fast and furious from Antarctica but thankfully blows through quickly over a short period. Yes, I had much to learn about the various wind patterns in New Zealand and what they meant in terms of the weather. Every weather pattern in this country is defined by the predominant wind. I had only been familiar with the warm, dry desert winds called the Santa Anas blowing into San Diego from Arizona.

Feisty Northwesterlies are the predominant wind in our area, coming from the tropical north, and often blows a gale where we live. Living in the Southern Hemisphere, one had to expect more wind as there is less land mass to deflect and absorb the air travelling across vast expanses of ocean. These winds generally tend to be on the warm side and not-so-biting cold or wet as the Southerlies, while Easterlies usually portend light, misty rain for days on end in the winter. Along with the winds, sunlight here is a frequent topic of conversation and how it affects everything from positioning a house to lathering on sunscreen. The hole in the ozone is purportedly right above us, thus putting one at higher risk for melanoma cancer than most other places in the world. As a point of interest, when one is building a house, or adding an extra story, it is not the neighbor's view which is protected, but the angle of sunlight and how this will affect surrounding properties.

A couple of months after arriving in Wairarapa, I decided to host my first dinner party in our modest rental home. It was with a sense of reserved pride in my cooking skills that I invited Aengus, his family and octogenarian grandmother next door to thank them for their kindness to our son and warmly welcoming us to Wairarapa. It's very fortunate that there's a wide variety of delicious organic produce and top quality abundant lamb, beef and fish at my fingertips in this area.

I decided I would make teriyaki flank steak tournedos and thusly set out to one of the local butchers in town to source the best cut of beef for my guests. Again, I was to receive the same confused look when I asked for two pounds of flank steak and was escorted to a map of a cow on the wall that detailed the various cuts of meat. Converting the pounds into kilos was easy enough and I asked the butcher to err generously on the amount I had ordered. Once I pointed to what I presumed to be the flank area of the cow, the butcher smiled at me and said, "Ah, you must be after some skirt steak then, eh?"

I nodded, trusting his interpretation, and was given a few slabs of what appeared to be a very thick, fleshy flank steak, not at all what I was really used to dealing with in California. So, I asked him if he would be kind enough to slice the meat across the grain into strips, and he replied, "Sweet as." (I had heard this expression now several times, and still waited for the sentence to be finished with what it was exactly sweet as . . . , sweet as what? Only to learn that this is yet another type of Kiwi slang, meaning "all good.")

So, off I return home to marinate the beef strips in plentiful of my own prepared teriyaki sauce, made with soy sauce, fresh ginger, garlic, brown sugar and some pineapple juice. Shortly before my guests arrived, I wrapped stringy bacon around each slice and twisted the strips into circles, secured with toothpicks. To save time, I forgave myself this one time and bought a box of instant mushroom risotto to accompany it and made a green salad tossed with my signature French vinaigrette. Shortly after my guests arrived, I placed the cooking tray under the grill for about three minutes on each side, as was my experience with this recipe, and then turned the oven off, covered the meat with foil, and let it rest.

The conversation flowed easily and it was delightful to get to know Aengus' grandmother next door as well, a very refined and well-traveled lady from what I learned chatting to her throughout the evening. Just before dinner was served, Jonathan turned to me and said, "So, Suzanne, rumor has it you want to start doing cooking classes here?"

"Oh well, we'll have to see about that," I answered modestly. "It's something I said I might like do once I'm all settled in my own house. It's been a dream, I suppose."

We sat down to dinner and passed around the platter of tournedos and all looked well, or so I thought with some relief. Rocking the knife to and fro, I cut into my steak with quite a bit of effort, which took me a bit off guard. I immediately looked around the table and noticed Jonathan, and his wife as well, chewing on a piece of the steak rather vigorously. I quickly glanced over at my husband and was pained to see he had a bit of frown appearing. Gingerly, I placed a small amount of the meat into my mouth, expecting it to be lovely and tender, but instead it had the consistency of thick, gnarly rope. I could barely chew it enough to swallow it safely and comfortably.

"Gosh," I said, with a glob of stringy meat in the corner of my mouth." I really must apologize for this dish. It's usually much more tender and not as tough and stringy for that matter. It doesn't taste at all like the flank steak I'm used to eating."

"By flank, you must be referring to our skirt steak, eh?" Jonathan asked. "Well, skirt steak in this country is usually used for slow cooking, as it's a relatively cheaper cut of meat. Also, the meat in the U.S. tends to be more tender, as your cattle are grain-fed there, whereas ours here are grass-fed, as in South America."

Cheaper cut of meat? Maybe I should have bought the Scotch fillets? Were they similar to filet mignon? I had no idea what some of these cuts of meat were at the local markets. Good God, I hoped I had not insulted them, and was feeling very embarrassed by this stage.

"I am so sorry! Honestly, I don't know about all these cuts. And to think my father comes from a farm with cattle trading and meatpacking. In fact, his occupation reads 'Butcher' on my birth certificate. I'm mortified. Honestly."

As it turned out, it was the damn store-bought boxed mushroom risotto dish, which didn't even have one fresh mushroom in it, which garnished the most culinary acclaims that evening. And to be honest, I have never bought another box of it again as it bears no resemblance to my own mushroom risotto. As for me and my efforts to impress our new friends with a California-inspired dish, I was humbled and sat quietly at the table for the rest of the meal, not daring to think what in God's name were their first impressions of my cooking, and how those skills, or seeming lack of them, would ever translate into leading cooking classes in my new life.

Sweet as . . . ?

NOT!

Ironically, a few years after that very memorable dinner party, flank steak is now a very trendy cut of meat amongst foodies here and I've introduced it to some wary guests in my cooking classes called "Let's Do Lunch." Thanks to celebrity Kiwi chef Al Brown, who described it in a magazine article as the most under-rated cut of beef used for barbecues in New Zealand, this cut of beef is readily available. But . . . there's still a need for a tri-tip cut of meat as marinated and sold at Seaside Market in Cardiff-by-the Sea, San Diego. Its sandwiches and steaks are famously a local addiction there, so much so it's referred to as "Cardiff Crack."

Real Estate – A Land of Landlords

OUR FIRST WEEK SETTLING INTO Wairarapa, one of our neighbors, Janet, stood knocking with enthusiasm at our back door and introduced herself as being a former nurse at the hospital, as well as being a good friend of the owner of our house. She was quick to take me under her wing and to offer valuable advice—whether I wanted it or not—on all types of things, ranging from buying and drying out firewood, to shopping at the local farmer's market, and finally to purchasing our first Kiwi home. The fact that her husband, George, was a real estate agent also happened to be most convenient. Soon, flyers were being dropped off at our doorstep detailing the more upscale properties in the area. In a town where the average decent property was selling for around $200,000 NZD, I was being shown the very rare ones asking over $500,000. I was soon to infer that local folk saw nothing but dollar signs on my forehead, as we had just moved from America, then the land of the almighty dollar, and my husband made his living as a surgeon: cha-ching, cha-ching.

One realtor actually confused the exchange rate with the English pound sterling at that time, informing me that our currency was worth three times the New Zealand dollar. It was assumed that everything quoted in New Zealand currency would be dirt-cheap for us converting it back into American dollars. Not so. Unfortunately for us, the New Zealand dollar had been climbing steadily in value since our move. It had been hovering around the sixty-cents mark when we first transferred American money over; each week, we witnessed our money decreasing cent by cent in exchange value. Living overseas makes one very conscious of exchange rate and I was eager to purchase property rather quickly, as home prices were climbing steadily as well. We had missed the "value" season back when we first visited in 2002, when the exchange rate was fifty cents to the American dollar and house prices had not yet begun to soar.

While not wishing to dwell on the negative side while our American dollar was not cashing in as optimally as it would have had we moved a few years earlier, it was reassuring to remind ourselves that our house in San Diego would not have sold at a hugely inflated price then, giving more American dollars to play with by 2004. Indeed, our San Diego house still remains the highest price paid for any house in that neighborhood to date, so I feel lucky indeed to have taken the leap of faith to sell it, rather than rent it out, just a few months before our move.

Looking for property in Wairarapa was left to me and became a full-time job and a real challenge as I was not in the least prepared for the landmine of nuances around New Zealand real estate transactions and law. I struggled to understand the business of buying and selling property. A multiple listing service here for properties is rare, which makes it necessary and time consuming to utilize the services of several real estate agencies at once to get a varied inventory of homes for sale. I was soon to learn that the agents were not responsible to make disclosures about defects or maintenance issues unless specifically asked by the prospective purchaser, a policy known as "buyer beware" and "due diligence." This has since changed by law, supposedly. Every question I would ask about the property was answered either, "I don't know," "Let me get back to you," or, "Better to ask a qualified builder." Often agents never did get back to me, even for a simple follow-up call. It was so unlike the American real estate agents I had dealt with in San Diego, who would have had the facts down cold about a particular property, including the year built, the local schools, any additions or alterations to the house, permits, type of heating, age of the roof, etc. Indeed, I truly questioned why there was a need at all for a real estate agent in house hunting as I have witnessed firsthand a total lack of professionalism in their willful deceit, greed and self-serving behavior.

The seller, or vendor in their real estate vernacular, is expected to pay for all advertising and marketing expenses on top of the commission paid to the agent. The vendor must detail all "chattels" being sold with the property and if not mentioned in the contract, it is assumed not included in the price. There were a few "quiet" listings I was shown, which meant that the property was not "really" for sale, or being actively marketed, but the owner would consider selling the property if his arbitrary price was met. Trying to get said price from the agent or the vendor was again another matter, as the burden fell on prospective buyers to name a price they would be willing to pay if keen on the house. Where was the transparency?

Many houses are sold by "auction" or "tender." What the heck? Why couldn't the vendor just name a price and go from there? No, it was all about driving the price up by competing bids for the same property. The whole practice seemed a trifle shady to me and all the rules around this type of sale acted as a big determent to even viewing these houses listed for sale by auction or tender.

My appointments to view houses for sale in the area, whether officially listed or not, were anything but a routine inspection and wound up becoming quite an adventure. One of the first properties I was shown, a fruit orchard, was a few miles out of town and was actually being sold as a "going concern" according to the agent. Apple and fruit trees were planted over a five-acre site with a small unpretentious stand at the end of the driveway from which the owner sold his produce. I walked around and in between many rows of trees as the owner described to me his growing and harvest season, the equipment he used which was stored in a nearby shed, the ride-on mower and shelves of spray cans filled with the necessary insecticide sprays to keep disease at bay. And all the while, I'm thinking, does he really think I'm seriously interested in taking this on? By the time we arrived at his nearby house, I was so overwhelmed by the amount of work he described to keep his business solvent, my head began to throb. There is no way in God's name that this is for me, I thought. No way.

While the notion of owning a productive and profitable fruit orchard did appeal to me in a romantically abstract Thomas Hardy kind of way, sober reality hit me in the face. I knew I was not destined to be a fruit orchard or any other type of farmer for that matter. Hell, he lost me when he spoke about "stone fruit." What? I had never heard peaches and nectarines being referred to as stone fruit until that day. Probably inferring my lack of enthusiasm, he tried hard to engage me and assure me that I could handle it and all would be good as gold.

The following weekend, my husband and I were driven to view a house on a hilly deer farm, another business property to which the owner was very committed and took great pride, but he had unfortunately just been diagnosed with lung cancer and had a poor prognosis. My husband and I were invited to climb aboard his quad bike and off we went on a tour of the entire operation, clambering over rocky stream beds and narrow ledges with steep drops looking down upon herds of deer who stared up at us with an air of caution. I held onto Paul's arm tightly for fear of flipping over and smiled at the ludicrous idea of considering this farm as a potential option for us. It was truly comedic in the sense that we were thought to be capable of harvesting velvet deer antlers and exporting them to China, along with the meat to Germany. Rather than house hunting, it felt like a leisurely afternoon game ride more than anything else. OK, enough of these hands-on going concerns we decided. My husband is hands-on all day working as a general surgeon after all.

After trying to make myself clearly understood that businesses were not our preferred method of entry into the housing market, I was brought to a house about ten minutes outside town that sat on ten acres with amazing, unobstructed views of the valley and mountains. The agent almost whispered to me to emphasize it was one of those "quiet" listings, a quirky New Zealand real estate term. The house itself was not spectacular in an architectural sense, but it was by far the best property I had seen since moving to Wairarapa. Paul and the family were very excited about the location, the views, and the acreage and we decided to waste no time and risk losing this opportunity. We would offer the full asking price as determined by the vendor. It was our thinking that this was just too good to pass up, and why haggle over a few dollars when this was well within our price range. So, without further hesitation, Paul and I signed the contract that same afternoon and immediately started discussing bathroom renovation plans.

The next day, our real-estate agent neighbor came by looking a bit grieved as he began to discuss the contract. He told us the vendor had increased the price by thirty thousand dollars. What?? I was shocked and slightly offended, to be quite honest. It was as if the vendor was thinking: well, hell, if they're willing to pay the asking price without question, we must not be asking enough then. Why not squeeze them for a wee bit more?

"At the end of the day, it's only thirty thousand dollars more, eh?" the agent offered.

"Well, at the end of the day, why don't you just take it off your commission, eh?" I suggested. "I don't know about you, but it takes me quite a bit of time and effort to earn, let alone save, thirty thousand dollars."

"Yes, but you have American dollars," he protested.

"That's not the point," I said, throwing my hands up in the air. "I just really resent the fact that this person is wanting to take complete advantage of us. It just doesn't sit well with me. I'm sorry, but the deal is off."

Big life lesson for me: NEVER offer the full asking price for anything, given that price is usually ALWAYS negotiable. It's just human nature: both the seller and the buyer wish to feel they are getting a bit of a deal, and that there is some sense of fairness in the deal. In the end, the seller will have always wanted a bit more, and the purchaser always to have paid a bit less.

And so it was back to making appointments with several agents to continue viewing properties. As we had some cash burning a hole in our pockets for the first time in years, I was interested in finding a coastal property as well, and began to look at Castlepoint, a wild east coast beach settlement about an hour's drive away. After a few trips out to the coast with my husband, he gently pointed out that we could just easily drive out there any time for a picnic and did not necessarily need a place there to "get away from it all," as we were already away from it all living in Wairarapa.

Indeed, Castlepoint is striking in its desolate beauty, but for the greater part of the year it is mostly windswept and cold with no facilities to recommend itself for any length of stay, which is exactly what the locals loved about the place. They couldn't justify any new commercial enterprises in the town to attract day visitors, say for example, a fish taco stand or small café. This utterly confounded me. I could have understood the sentiments had one been visiting the area from a congested urban city life, but going to their holiday homes, or bach in Kiwi jargon, from Wairarapa was not escaping anything, only taking it to the sea: the same faces, the same talk, the same ol', same ol'.

My husband, addressing my city-girl roots, began to encourage me to look for a place in Wellington, something more urban. It was, after all, a city and the capital of New Zealand, with cultural and social activities to highly recommend itself as a fun urban "getaway" from Wairarapa. And, one of the most attractive things about living in Wairarapa is that there is a train that leaves several times a day to make the hour-and-a-half journey to Wellington. Sweet as.

Soon I found a two-bedroom townhome near Parliament. It reminded me of the trendy townhouses in the Paddington area of Sydney and was easy walking distance to the main shopping area of Wellington, Lambton Quay. An offer was made and accepted by the vendor, a terrific price I thought for what I was getting, and all very straightforward according to the snazzy young real estate agent. As there is no escrow service in New Zealand, the vendor and purchaser must both employ the services of a solicitor who deals in property transactions to review and confirm the contract.

A few days later, I received a phone call from our local solicitor in Wairarapa to inform me that she had reviewed the contract and, while doing a title search, learned there was a "Treaty of Waitangi" lien on the property. What the heck was that, I enquired. When I informed the agent of this news from the solicitor, she brushed it off as if it were a mere inconvenience, nothing for me to worry about at all. Many properties in New Zealand had these "Treaty" liens on them, she advised me, and most settled out of court for cash payouts. Our solicitor, on the other hand, was a bit more adamant that further investigations be made, and gave me the contact details of the leader of the Waitangi Tribunal in Wellington to discuss the legal implications of the lien. Now I had NO idea that this tribunal is a very big deal here, and the fact that I could speak directly and effortlessly to the leader was indeed remarkable.

This solicitor was truly doing her job well, and I am grateful to her to this day. I was to learn that this lien was not something to take lightly at all, and could negatively affect the resale value of the property in the future. And if it were to be repossessed by a Māori treaty claim, there would be a chance I might not be reimbursed the full purchase price. Again, I felt taken advantage of in the New Zealand real estate arena. This contract was reluctantly canceled soon after that information was gleaned, despite the protests from the agent, who continued to insist that

I was withdrawing from a fantastic opportunity to get into the Wellington market. Uh . . . no, thanks!

A few weeks later, while taking the train into Wellington, I stared out the window across the glistening bluish-green waters of the harbor over to the Oriental Bay area, which was bathed in sunlight and looked so happy to me. I sighed, thinking, if only . . . . . Upon arrival, another agent with whom I was working met me in front of the railway station and asked, "Suzanne, have you ever thought about Oriental Bay?"

"Of course," I answered. "Who hasn't? But there's no way I can afford anything over there, honestly."

"Well, let's go have a look at this apartment that is set to come on the market shortly. You never know. There might just be a way."

I remained circumspect as we drove across the city and towards Oriental Bay, amongst the most prestigious addresses in New Zealand. The anxious thoughts swimming around my head were not positive. Surely the property must be dingy, and up some side street with no views, as everything else would most certainly be out of my price range.

And so it was we drove up a road off Oriental Parade and up a steep hill towards the towering Catholic monastery that commands an impressive location, perched as it is overlooking the entire harbor and city. Immediately, I sat up in the car and began to feel hopeful, and at the very least, wishful.

She parked the car, and we walked towards a rather boring, large rectangular building that opened into a tired-looking lobby. We took the elevator up to the eighth floor, and once the door was opened and I looked inside, I held my breath. The views held me captive and I wanted to scream with joy, "Yes. Yes. This is it!! Oh my God!!!"

I was suddenly transported back to my little love nest with Paul in our single days on the Filbert Steps on Telegraph Hill in San Francisco. This was surely too good to be true. Then I brought myself back to the present and had a walk around the one-bedroom apartment. The green shag carpet could be replaced; the walls repainted, the bubbly ceiling scraped and plastered and the bathroom could have a bit of a makeover. It was true that I had wanted a two-bedroom place for the family to stay, but the overall feel of the place was good, and there was adequate room for our purposes. This was it! No question. I had to have it, but tried hard to conceal my enthusiasm from the agent.

Onto the asking price, which I had since learned was indeed very arbitrary in New Zealand real estate transactions. Instinctively, I made what I considered a fair offer, then signed the contract with a few conditions before boarding the afternoon train back to Wairarapa. I simply could not let this fantastic opportunity slip. My husband trusted my judgment completely and signed the contract without an inspection of the property and it was hand-delivered to our solicitor the next day.

Thorough as ever, she rang me with her concerns. It was a "company share" apartment, which meant what exactly? Well, there were certain conditions, one of which included not being permitted to rent it out as one might want to do with an "investment" property. I learned that many New Zealand folk, even down to the janitor at our local hospital, owned properties for both investment and tax purposes, as the mortgage interest of the primary residence in New Zealand is not tax deductible, only on investment properties. These apartments in the building I was buying into were all owner occupied. Not a problem, as we wanted it solely for our own use. The fact that it was structured as a "company share" also meant that banks might not loan as much on them as well. Not a problem, as this was to be paid for in cash. All good. The vendor, who lived next door, was anxious to sell as her husband was very ill and she wanted to put the money towards a beach house she had her eyes on about an hour out of town. I was assured that the "hole" in the wall she had made between her two-bedroom corner apartment and the one for sale, would be repaired back to its original condition as a one-bedroom property. The contract became unconditional, and we had a settlement date in early November. Yeah!!

To this day, I thank God for the luxury of owning a little slice of heaven in this fabulous city and feel so grateful every time I am down there to use our apartment and share it with friends and family from overseas.

Now that I had the city pad organized, the hunt continued for the permanent family home in Wairarapa. Our neighbor, George, worked hard to find us the right house after the last debacle, but nothing satisfactory was forthcoming. Soon after buying the apartment in Wellington, I began to look at vacant lots, called sections here, and to discuss the process of designing and building a home with a few recommended building contractors in town.

I was taken to a section that was on top of a hill with almost nine acres and postcard views of the twisting valley river below and distant snow-capped mountains. It was all I had dreamed about for a building site in New Zealand, and here it was for sale, and we could afford it. Well, after a month or so of haggling, a price was agreed upon and the contract signed and processed by the same, thorough solicitor. Our settlement date was to be the same week as the apartment in Wellington. It was all go. We now owned a city apartment and a country property. But, we still needed a place to live in a couple of months' time, when our hospital rental house would no longer be available to us.

The contract was no sooner unconditional when George appeared at our door, certain he had found us the "right" house, up the road from our rental home, with gorgeous views as well. Within a few days, our offer was accepted, and we were signing a contract to buy a house, with six garages, on two acres of land. All of a sudden, we were "property owners" in New Zealand, and months of my tossing and turning and worrying were coming to an end as we strived to put down roots. Again, this was something we could never have conceived nor practically achieved while working as we did in San Diego in above average, salaried positions.

We had lived in a modest tract home in Encinitas, but it had unobstructed views over a lagoon and out to the ocean and it bordered one of the most exclusive addresses in California, Rancho Santa Fe. This is what commanded such a high sale price in the end. Our children went to the same public schools as these kids, and I remembered one day when Alex came home and asked, "Mom . . . how come we don't have *property*?

A few of his friends did not apparently own just homes . . . they owned "*property.*" Honestly!

So, I looked at his sweet little face and without apologies or hesitation explained, "Well, Alex, you like to go on ski vacations in the winter, right? And travel to different countries during your school breaks, right? And you like your mommy not working and free to drive you, instead of a nanny, to and from school and all your activities and school trips, right? Well, honey, that's where our money goes and that's why we do not have property."

He nodded thoughtfully and then disappeared out the garage door on his bike to explore the canyon with friends.

Indeed, the more we earned in San Diego, the more expenses there seemed to be, in the way of increasing health insurance premiums, mortgage payments, property taxes, exorbitant medical malpractice insurance and not to mention we had university tuitions looming ahead of us for our two teenagers; you name it. I felt as if we were guinea pigs in a cage, running incessantly on the exercise wheel and getting no further ahead.

We had been living in New Zealand about three months when we were informed the freight container storing our life possessions had arrived safely in Wellington and passed customs without any drama. As we were to be living in the rental home another three months, storage was arranged in Wellington.

To tell you the truth, after not seeing our hitherto cannot-live-without-stuff for quite some time, I was not missing any of the contents in the slightest. It was rather a case of "out of sight, out of mind." In fact, I couldn't have cared less if the whole damn container had tumbled off the ship and disappeared somewhere in transit crossing the South Pacific, as I would have been spared the formidable ordeal and aggravation of unpacking, along with addressing the flood of memories associated with the contents. That being said, I must admit that it is rather comforting in my new life to have some familiar furnishings, linens, and dishes from San Diego as the cost to replace these would have been exorbitant in New Zealand, where it seems almost everything is imported from overseas.

Over the twelve years that we have now lived here, property around the Auckland area has skyrocketed with more and more overseas buyers seeing great value in owning a piece of the housing market here. Why wouldn't they, with such advantages to investors as no capital gains or stamp duty? New Zealand is a vastly underpopulated country with expansive areas upon which to build a new life, and all at bargain prices compared to many desirable spots in the western world. Truly, I am so grateful to be living here and so far removed from all the misfortunes and general worries and heartaches in the world. New Zealand is without a doubt a sanctuary at the bottom of the world. And it just keeps getting better and feeling more like home all the time.

Holidays

OUR FIRST CHRISTMAS IN NEW ZEALAND was looming and I still had no concrete plans about how we would spend it, but it all came together one afternoon in late October in Wellington. I was browsing through a sale rack at a women's clothing store when a conversation blossomed with the woman standing next to me about the high cost of clothing in this country. A sideward glance and a smile ensued along with a question about my accent. I quickly learned that she lived in Tasmania but was originally from Wairarapa of all places and was in Wellington to attend a midwifery conference and to visit her aging parents. Soon we were telling our life stories in ten minutes and introductions were made.

Tasmania? I was instantly intrigued and told her I had hoped to make a trip there someday, whereby my new friend Sally responded by graciously extending an invitation to visit her anytime. The wheels started turning in my head, as my friend Julie in Sydney had told me she and the family were planning to spend Christmas in the UK with her mother, and that her house in Paddington would be free for us to use. Soon a plan developed . . . we would fly to Sydney, spend a few days with her before they took off on their trip, then take the overnight *Spirit of Tasmania* ferry on Christmas Eve to Tasmania, where we would celebrate Christmas day with Sally and her family. Any Christmas decorations I had shipped were still in storage and being far away from family and friends, I wanted a bit of a distraction, as we were not in our own home yet.

As it so happened, I had given away most of my Christmas and other holiday decorations upon the suggestion of my husband, who had believed that Christmas wouldn't be celebrated in the same fashion as it was in the Northern Hemisphere. Well, he was a bit off the mark on that one because there was clearly an expectation from locals that we would be American Christmas personified, and many professed an envy of the American decorations they had envisaged we were bringing over with us. Oh, the pressure to have this Martha Stewart-type living room filled with holly, evergreens, twinkling lights, a festive over-the-top table setting and decorations, not to mention the designer Christmas tree. Oven-roasted turkey with all the trimmings was very much a yearning as well, though it was summer time. Australia was indeed proving the answer to all my holiday woes.

We landed in Sydney carrying newly purchased Christmas stockings which were to be filled with goodies from the Bondi Westfield Mall, near to where we were staying in Paddington. Our teenaged daughter, thrilled to be back in a real mall, darted up and down escalators to different floors giddy with shopping fever. To add to our excitement, our former San Diego neighbors who had moved to the Gold Coast a few years prior to our move had decided to join us in Sydney after our trip to Tasmania.

On Christmas Eve, we boarded the *Spirit of Tasmania* in Sydney, only to find it rather modestly appointed and lacking in any festive ambience or Christmas cheer. My husband had to remind me that this was a ferry service after all and not a cruise ship. Undaunted, we made the best of the overnight sailing, and plundered our Christmas stockings after breakfast before disembarking in the Tasmanian port city, Devonport. I had arranged to meet Sally and her group at a national park about an hour outside Hobart, where she had booked cottages for Christmas. After a few hours' drive, we arrived to quite an authentic Dickensian affair in that we had no electricity or running water in the cottages and the toilet facilities consisted of a communal outhouse accessed across a brook about one hundred feet or so from the cottages but . . . there was stuffed roast turkey, a huge ham and Christmas crackers awaiting us when we arrived at dusk. After the introductions were made, we were presented with a large bag filled with thoughtful and useful wrapped presents and told to pick one from the lucky dip which quickly broke the ice and made us feel warmly welcomed to this group of male and female midwives and their families. I almost expected a toast to Tiny Tim at any moment . . . .

After a meander around the park lake on Boxing Day, trying to spot platypus and wombats, we drove to the B & B Sally had booked us for the night outside Hobart. It was owned by a French couple and sat high on the hill with panoramic views overlooking the Hobart harbor, which proved a wonderful spot to appreciate the unique geography of this city. The next morning, which was Boxing Day in the Northern Hemisphere, I turned on the television expecting to hear reports of the annual Sydney to Hobart yacht race only to be bombarded with news of a devastating tsunami that wiped out large areas in Indonesia and Thailand. Our morning coffee was indeed marred as we sat high and safe on a hill in Hobart and listened to reports of holidaymakers vanishing into the wave that hit some of the most popular resorts. Soon we were receiving anxious phone calls from family and friends in California enquiring about our safety, mistakenly thinking Tasmania was in the affected region as well.

Later that morning, we took off on our three-night tour of the east coast, stopping first for a tour of Port Arthur, one of the largest convict settlements in Australia in the mid–1800s. In fact, about three-quarters of present-day Tasmanians supposedly are descended from convicts, a history that folk prefer not to talk about. It's an inheritance that is referred to by some as "The Stain." Here were exiled the most-hardened and brutal of prisoners, many of whom were deemed too bad for imprisonment on the mainland and an experiment with psychological versus physical punishment was implemented as well. The convicts did terrible things to get there and did terrible things once there. Port Arthur was also known as the prison for young boys, some as young as nine years old, convicted of such minor offenses as stealing a toy. The brutality of this settlement was renowned and greatly feared as a prison sentence as it came with little hope of escape, situated as it was on the Tasman peninsula surrounded by what was rumored by administration to be shark-infested waters.

Undeterred by half-starved dogs and guards heavily patrolling the 30km isthmus leading to the mainland, escapes were nonetheless tempted and met with only few successes. One famous account revolves around a young man, George "Billy" Hunt, who was quite creative in his attempt to flee by using the hide of a kangaroo to disguise himself and hop across the isthmus. Mistaken for a real kangaroo, he was soon being fired upon by the hungry guards, anxious to add some sustenance to their meager food rations. Fearing for his life, he threw off his kangaroo charade and received 150 lashes upon surrender.

Port Arthur is now one of Tasmania's largest tourist attractions, and I for one felt a sense of discomfort paying to see a site imbued with so much unsavory history, including much physical and mental hardship with the resulting utter hopelessness amongst its former inhabitants.

I learned about the juvenile convicts sent to nearby Point Puer, the first British Empire boy's prison. These supposed convicts were doomed to hard labor and untold acts of punishment during their young years into adulthood, with no chance of having a normal life of a first love, marriage and family, in what was to be a dismal future. The air of melancholy and desolation emanating from the prison walls and grounds struck me as we were led to view the mass graves on the Isle of the Dead. I have no doubt the stories describing frequent ghost sightings and hauntings reported in this settlement are true, given its brutal past during these early days of Australia's less than honorable history of convict settlements and murderous relations with the indigenous people. Nowhere were race relations noted to be worse than in Tasmania where "The Black War" of the 1820s killed 1000 Aborigines and "The black line" was an attempt by 2200 whites, ten percent of the population in 1830, to sweep Aborigines from the island.

This history aside, Tasmania is a beautiful country to visit with very kind and welcoming folk, though no sightings of the famed Tasmanian Devil were noted. We enjoyed the remaining time driving up the east coast back to Devonport, where I was happy to board the *Spirit of Tasmania* back to Sydney to meet up with our friends and bring in our first New Year living in the Southern Hemisphere and to welcome in 2005.

Sydney was bustling on New Year's Eve, with people scampering all over Paddington to and from the local gourmet markets to purchase seafood, salads and fresh-baked goodies to fill picnic baskets—hampers—and bring in the New Year by its famous harbor setting. Our San Diego friend, Brett, had arranged for us all to join his uncle on his yacht for the evening and he had left early that morning to secure an anchor somewhere in the sea of boats already assembled there for the festivities.

The rest of us were left in charge of supplies and libations and got busy making pasta salads, sandwiches and packing the liquid provisions to bring on board the boat. The plan was to make our way to the water taxi stand in Circular Quay and then get ferried over to the sailboat.

Well, it all sounded simple enough, though when we arrived at the Sydney Opera House, the whole area was cordoned off in an attempt to keep order and celebrate the alcohol-free notion of First Night. A wonderful concept indeed, First Night, but one I was nowhere near ready to embrace at this time as bottles of beer and champagne clanked happily away in our bags. Security fences were heavily patrolled by local police and privately paid guards, with check points at every entrance to the area to ensure no alcohol was being smuggled into the grounds, thus posing a huge dilemma for us as the only way to the water taxis was through this restricted area. Quickly deciding that honestly is the best policy, I approached a police officer and pleaded our case as best I could and was rewarded with an official escort through security and over to the water taxi station, only to be informed that the taxis were not running due to a heightened terrorist alert.

"What? How are we supposed to get to our boat?" we asked.

Brett's wife, Kim, immediately got on her cell phone and rang her husband. We were assured he would ask a neighboring party with a dinghy to come and collect us, but we would have to make our way down to the pier near the steps closest to the Sydney Opera House. This meant having to go through security once again, and now there was no kind police officer in sight.

When we reached the checkpoint, we were asked: "Do you have any grog?"

"Of course I do," I replied. "There are two very thirsty men waiting on a boat for us since early morning.

"I'm sorry," he informed us. "But this is a venue with strictly no alcohol permitted. At all. You will have to dump it here," he said, pointing to a nearby bin, filled with unopened bottles and cans of beer and spirits.

I had to think fast. I motioned to Kim, Paul and the kids to move out of the queue until another solution was sourced, which it soon was in the form of a woman at another nearby checkpoint, who just so happened to own the security company. She listened patiently while I explained our plight and the fact that water taxis were not running, and soon gave us the clearance needed to go through the gates to walk to the Opera steps on the other side of the venue. Yeah!!! Hallelujah! What a hassle! Soon we were fetched by a man in a three-person dingy, who had to make several trips to and fro to ferry us out to our sailboat, which sat happily bobbing amidst hundreds of its kind, anchored in the harbor.

Ahhhhh . . . . It was an absolutely gorgeous late afternoon, and the sense of revelry and anticipation in the air was infectious.

Sydney Harbor resembled a huge aqueous parking lot on a big sale day, filled as it was to capacity with yachts of all sizes and appointment. Every bit of green in the surrounding public parks was covered in colorful blankets and chairs, with picnic baskets of every description overflowing with epicurean delights.

We soon set about getting our own picnic underway, washed down with chilled champagne and wine. Even though a quick dip in the sea was inviting, no one was swimming. We were soon warned best not to take the chance, as this area was known to be popular with bull sharks, with maybe a Great White amongst them. Ah well, there were plenty of other distractions on the sea to keep us entertained until the first set of fireworks was scheduled to go off at 9 p.m., so that families with young children would be catered to firstly.

And it was truly a spectacular show!!

We had over two hours to go before the grand show at midnight, and to our utter dismay, we had finished all the grog. Honestly! And not even the slightest remote chance of buying any more. *Oh for a draught of vintage! that hath been cool'd a long age in the deep delvéd earth . . .* but none was to be forthcoming. Booze, booze everywhere, and not a drop to drink. If there had been a supply boat out there in that harbor that night, no doubt a tidy fortune could have been made by that enterprising individual. Clearly, it was time to rehydrate with the plentiful bottles of water we had carted along, and by midnight, everyone was really happily sober as the dazzling display of fireworks bombarded the skies. In all the 4th of July celebrations experienced in my life, both on the east and west coasts of the USA, I have never witnessed such a breathtaking pyrotechnic show of color and form, the most impressive being the waterfall of fire lights pouring down from the Sydney Harbor Bridge into the sea at midnight. In a word: mesmerizing.

Upon our captain's orders, we hung tight in our spot as boats clamored back to port under the bridge. Ours was a small vessel, about twenty-six feet or so, and with nine of us crammed on board, it most likely would not have performed safely in the resulting swell. The night wore on, and soon we began finding places to get horizontal and wait it out. It was dawn when I heard Brett taking orders from his uncle to hoist the sail, and with the motor humming softly, we negotiated our way back towards the Opera House, where we had boarded over twelve hours earlier. The sea was flat, mirroring the buildings bordering it and shimmering with dazzling colors as the night faded away to a crisp dawn.

It was with a grateful heart that I came up on deck, somewhat disheveled but with a clear head, and watched the first sun rise of 2005 cast its orange and rosy hues over the skies to the east of the Opera House and the Sydney Harbor Bridge. What a sight! A perfect postcard picture, my husband would soon announce to us all. We hugged our San Diego friends farewell, and then set upon trying to flag down a taxi to take us back to Paddington. This proved a near impossible task as many of them had been pre-booked for weeks, and were in no need of extra fares. Hotels and clubs were bustling with business at six in the morning, doing a roaring after-hours party trade that was to last until noon. Well, those party days were well past me, and I pitied those inside the sore heads to be had in a few hours.

This was the best New Year's Eve to date. EVER!! My husband Paul was correct in a sense to assume the holidays are celebrated here in a different manner. Christmas, being in the middle of summer, is an extremely busy time for the farmers, who are making hay, getting stock sold off and desperately trying to keep the land irrigated in the long, dry summers of late. Less is more here, and a little Christmas decoration goes a long way. It is less frantic and less commercial, with more emphasis put on reconnecting with family and friends, at the beach preferably, and sharing food with lots of bubbly, strawberries, seafood and wine. There is a rush to get practical things in order and completed because this country shuts down for about two weeks around Christmas, and many people take some holiday leave and head for the beach. At least it feels like no business is getting done. The only business is holiday business. Cars packed to capacity with holiday gear hit the roads everywhere and head towards the beach, lakes or mountain "baches."

Kiwis on the move. God!! I love it here . . . am I a lucky person or not to awaken in such a paradise as is New Zealand? Here the normal vacation package is paid four weeks. Add in all the public holidays here and one can easily enjoy over five weeks' paid leave. Why the United States doesn't join most of the Christian western world and make the 26th December, Boxing Day, a holiday is beyond me. And Easter is a four-day weekend here with Good Friday and Easter Monday both being legal holidays. Gotta love it!

As for my lack of American decorations, I have made do with Kiwi fare and it is just fine. Why should we try to emulate an *Olde* English experience when we are living way south of the equator? Paul does his best to be adamant in that only local flora and fauna be used to get a sense of the Christmas season here and so, replacing evergreen and holly, my mantel and vases are filled with the New Zealand Christmas tree blossoms from the native Pohutukawa tree. But it is quite convenient that one of my friends here sells traditional Christmas trees . . . and I am gifted one every year. We decorate with familiar Christmas ornaments, each one telling its story. And there is still lots of Christmas cheer, and gratitude, in my heart. And a stuffed, oven-roasted turkey continues to be proudly placed on my table when we are all home in Wairarapa, as some traditions one just cannot compromise.

It truly is . . . All good.

A Home of Our Own

WE ARRIVED BACK TO WAIRARAPA to begin a new year in a new house, our house, just up the road from our rental home, and we felt very excited to be putting down roots after six months of itinerant living. A moving truck packed tightly with all our U.S. possessions arrived early one morning and the dreaded unpacking and sorting began and continued over a couple of weeks.

I was both pleasantly surprised that most of our household goods survived the trans-Pacific voyage and horrified to unpack so many material possessions. How was I going to find a place for all these things? My sense of excessive consumerism was further impressed upon me when a woman from my morning tea group stopped by one day to help me unpack some boxes. As I carefully unwrapped all my Lenox china and wine glasses, it became painfully apparent that she was not used to so many different glasses assigned to so many different beverages. This one was for white wine, that one for red wine, this one for martinis, that one for margaritas.

"Good Lord!" she said. "I just use the one type of glass for wine and another for water and fizzy drinks. This is just so American."

Aside from feeling embarrassed at the sheer volume of dishes, platters and glasses I had accumulated over the years, I was slightly disgusted with myself for the way I had spent money without a thought on these things in California. See it, need it, must buy it NOW was my shopping mentality back then. When I started in on the boxes of clothing from my former days in San

Diego, I was shocked to find many with price tags still on them, unworn and by now totally out of fashion or not in New Zealand fashion.

Immediately, I summoned the children and instructed them to go through all their clothes and decide which things they no longer wanted or needed. In an effort to make this task painless, I told them it would help the victims of the tsunami and we were doing our bit to help out in this catastrophe. It did help me at least to think that many clothes and household items which had had their day with me would now be enjoyed by someone else. Bags and bags of hitherto treasured belongings were carted off to the local Salvation Army, and still there was this sense of over-entitlement, as I looked around at all the things I insisted on keeping. I do regret to this day though, placing my Donegal-tweed long cape coat in that box of discarded clothes and can only hope someone is enjoying its warmth today.

Though this house was ours, in the sense that we bought it, it was meant to be a holding ground until we built a house on the section we had purchased a few months after arriving. It might have been regarded as the dream house of many in our town, sited as it was on two acres with sweeping views of the local mountains, but the floor plan was quirky, the heating systems varied and complex, and it just did not have the right feel to me. All else was humming along well; Paul was settled in and regarded well at the hospital, Alex was enjoying his *Lost Boys* experience at his boarding school, Catherine was doing OK for the most part and our social life was full of new and fascinating diversions.

Our hospital was always in need of locum doctors and soon we were hosting dinners to welcome foreigners from the States, Australia and Europe to our new home as we had enjoyed upon our arrival. These temporary transplants breathed life into what might have been a rather lackluster existence in our town. One such locum surgeon heralded from the American Midwest and, aside from stature, he was larger than life in his generosity and hospitality. Frequently, he hosted happy hours in a lovely restaurant situated in the middle of our town park, Café Cecille, and many of the hospital staff were only too willing to have a reason to celebrate TGIF gatherings there where the wine of the week was on half-price special and drunk amongst lots of chatter. If one lingered around, there was always the opportunity to stay on for a meal hosted by said surgeon Dr. Bob.

It was reminiscent of my younger days as a nurse at Highland Hospital in Oakland, where hospital staff would congregate after work for a session of Liver Rounds, otherwise known as a "piss-up" here, and heal all the wounds of the week. Not only did the workers at ground floor Wairarapa Hospital appear at these sessions, but often the hospital manager and the CEO would stop by as well to enjoy the camaraderie and laughter in neutral circumstances.

I was very lucky to have met an anesthetist, Kasia, from Amsterdam doing a locum for a year at our hospital. She and I clicked immediately at a going away party for another locum surgeon and often met in Wellington for some needed weekend city distractions and culture. She was an avid cyclist and she soon encouraged me to join her for bike rides around the country roads. We are still great friends to this day, but I often wish she didn't have to return home as it would have been great to have her living in the area.

But . . . as is life, cracks started to appear, very subtly at first. It was about this time that our daughter began having ongoing problems at her private all-girls' school and pleaded with us to change schools and begin the following year at the public, co-ed high school across town. She was considered to be a bit too stroppy for the conservative campus environment, and her independent ways did not sit well with some of the more sedate and old school teachers, one of whom should have retired from her post ages ago. Catherine complained that this one particular teacher always singled her out as the only one chatting inappropriately in class, or passing notes, or being tardy, and Catherine insisted she was always the fall guy as the teacher displayed an obvious dislike of Americans.

Once this particular teacher had the class do a report on New Zealand weather systems and Catherine wrote about tornados. She was immediately singled out and scolded for her ignorance as the teacher informed the class that New Zealand never experienced tornados. That evening, as if by an act of God, a city on the west coast of the South Island, Greymouth, was gutted by, you've guessed it, a tornado.

The teacher began her class the next morning by saying, "Class, I stand corrected . . . there are the very occasional tornados in New Zealand." All the same, no direct apologies were forthcoming to Catherine.

The final insult happened one morning as I was typing away at home doing an article for our local newspaper on tourism in the area. I received a hysterical call from Catherine as she relayed through emotional sobbing that she had been ordered off the bus in the middle of town enroute for an orientation tour of the school where Alex attended. Catherine had had her name on the list, and had been checked off by a teacher as she boarded the bus, but later the teacher must have recalled hearing something about Catherine's future plans to change schools.

"Is Catherine Tunney on this bus?" the teacher yelled, waving the list in the air as they neared the roundabout at the edge of town.

"Yes, Miss. Here," Catherine answered, thinking she had forgotten to put a tick by her name on the list.

"What are you doing on this bus?" she screamed. "Stop the bus!" she yelled to the bus driver, who initially refused. "Stop the bus NOW!"

Then turning her attentions to Catherine, "Why are you on this bus? You know full well that you are not supposed to be on this tour. You won't even be attending our school next year. You cheeky, cheeky girl. Get off this bus now. Immediately!"

Catherine at first thought she was joking, as it was preposterous to think she was actually being thrown off the bus at the top end of town, a fair walk from her school grounds. "Miss," she began, "I don't know for sure if I am changing schools yet. I wanted to have a tour to make up my mind."

"Get off this bus NOW."

Catherine walked slowly to the front and stepped off the bus, humiliated and fighting back tears. The bus roared off without her as she tried to keep face by laughing and waving to the girls as they looked on behind the windows in bewilderment. When she rang me and recounted what had happened, I asked her to stay put and told her I was on my way. Never bothering to change out of my exercise pants, I dashed into the car and raced off to collect her and headed straight to the principal's office. Truly, I had had enough of this outright harassment and belittling of my daughter and felt it needed to be addressed at once with this teacher held accountable for such unacceptable behavior.

The headmaster was not available, I was told, as he was meeting the girls at the boy's school for the tour but I was welcome to make an appointment to see him the next day, should I wish. No, thank you; I wanted to speak to him directly and urgently. I insisted he must have a cell phone and that he be contacted at once. Other staff, hearing my high-pitched demands, started coming into the corridor to see what the ruckus was. I was soon told that he would return in an hour and would meet me in his office.

I decided to drive home with Catherine and tidy myself up a bit when I ran into the deputy headmistress who lived close by to the school. Obviously she must have been alerted of the incident and asked to stand in and calm the situation before the headmaster arrived, and so waved me down as I approached the school gate. Into the car she jumped, and I pulled over and began to cry.

What is the problem with this teacher? I asked. She has had it in for my daughter since day one. Why is she let away with this behavior? While acknowledging that Catherine was not perfect, I told her I had had input from other parents that this particular teacher does indeed have favorites and it wasn't only my daughter who suffered in the class.

In the meantime, I had called my husband at work and he agreed to meet with the headmaster as well at lunchtime as he too was gravely concerned about this latest incident at school. Over a cup of tea during the next hour, the headmaster listened rather aloofly as Catherine relayed what had happened on the bus and then had the audacity to support the teacher, insisting she was most respected in the school, and that surely Catherine must be somewhat exaggerating the incident a wee bit, as teens are prone to do. This attitude did not sit well with Paul at all, and soon apologies were made to Catherine and a promise to hold a meeting with the teacher to review these events. Catherine walked back to class feeling somewhat vindicated, until the next morning at school assembly when, after the headmaster finished his morning address, he turned and looked down at Catherine and said: "And Catherine, about yesterday's incident. You know, and I know, that you were not supposed to be on that bus."

It was soon thereafter an appointment was arranged with the public school headmaster, and Catherine was enrolled for her junior year at the co-ed college (high school) across town. Catherine only attended a year there, but it was a good year as it gave her a bit of a respite from the regimented environment of the other private all-girls' boarding school. She felt she wasn't being academically challenged enough in that few of her peers had University aspirations, which is a given for most U.S. students.

A friend of mine, another South African, suggested Wanganui Collegiate school as she had friends with children who did very well there. Catherine overheard her accolades and went about contacting the headmaster about placement there. It was with surprise that my husband received an e-mail from him soon thereafter informing us that there was an opening for Catherine.

"What in God's name is this about?" Paul asked me. "She is not changing schools again. How is this going to look on her transcripts? Is she writing a guide to New Zealand secondary schools or what?"

I tried to cajole him to agree to at least let me drive her there and do a tour as suggested by the headmaster and even told him that Prince Edward had done a stint there which added to the school's bragging rights. He still was not impressed.

After spending a few hours there on campus, there was no doubt in my mind that this was the perfect fit for her. A few weeks later, we packed up the car and Catherine enrolled as a full-time boarder at age sixteen and never looked back. Wanganui Collegiate school proved to be the answer to all her woes.

A Long Way Home

C LOSE TO 8 A.M. ONE APRIL Sunday morning, less than a year after arriving in New Zealand, the phone rang next to my bed and I was surprised to hear my brother's voice at the other end calling from Minnesota. As I wiped the sleep from my eyes, he told me that our mother had just passed away in the hospital a few minutes ago.

"What?" I screamed into the receiver. "Mom is dead? No! When? What? Is there going to be a . . . funeral or something?"

"Well, yes," he answered tersely. "That is what usually happens, Suzanne, when someone dies."

Ahhh, thanks for that, Bro'.

A day that was supposed to begin with a bike ride with my new friend Kasia to a nearby winery for lunch now became consumed with plans to get back quickly and affordably to the United States, and it honestly remains a bit of a blur to this day. I remember my husband and son running from the kitchen into the bedroom in response to my screeching tears and putting their arms around me in the bed. I asked Paul to call my friend to cancel the bike ride, as I was due to meet her shortly at her house.

What to do now? Should we all go back to the States for the funeral? Who was going to organize it all? The kids were doing mid-term tests, and the other surgeon was out of town on leave, leaving only Paul to toe the line for general surgery at the hospital. I took my cup of coffee and went out to the deck off our kitchen and stared at the horses frolicking below in the paddock across from our house, and was reminded of my mother's passion for horses. Her life was now over, with all its trials and tribulations finally put to rest with her.

This sudden event was a sobering reminder of how far away we were from family and close friends in the United States. Not only was the flight around thirteen hours, one had to figure in the amount of time it would take to get to the airport, another two hours, connecting flights to Dallas to meet my family and all the airport time. Not to mention the hours scouring the internet and making phone calls to verify flights and costs and on and on.

That mournful day for me was spent mostly on the phone trying to make arrangements to fly over to Texas, where my mother had been living with my younger sister. I talked at length with my only relative in the Southern Hemisphere, Kate, who lives in Melbourne with her Australian husband and with whom I had lived a couple of years in Northern Ireland to finish school when my parents moved to Dublin. She of all people would understand the pain suffered at the sudden loss of a parent as her own father, my uncle, died at age forty after having a sudden heart attack. Many hours that sad day I sat outside, staring trance-like at the horses grazing and prancing in the fields below me. The space around me felt barren, empty. I felt my mother to be so gone. I could not feel her spirit or presence despite how hard I tried to summon it. Nothing. She was truly done with this world, without a doubt.

No matter how I might have envisaged this moment, losing my mother, I don't believe I was ever really ready for that moment when it actually occurred. Is anyone? There was so much more of life I wanted my mother to be a part of, such as being there when my children graduated high school and university, attending their weddings, maybe even becoming a great-grandmother one day but sadly this was not to be. Who would I call now to confide my worries, to chat, to joke or just to unload and catch up? The one person, aside from my husband, who always listened, always forgave and always had time for me was now gone.

It was decided best that I go back to the States alone, until Catherine insisted that she too must accompany me to say goodbye to Grandma. I booked flights online to leave the next morning, and learned there were no special last minute or bereavement fares from New Zealand, so we paid over $6000.00 for two economy round-trip fares to Dallas, Texas.

The Qantas flight was overbooked, but luckily Catherine and I were assigned seats in the bulkhead, giving us space and a bit of extra leg room to stretch out during the twenty or so hours of flight time ahead of us, including a stopover at LAX. Not long into the crowded flight, a couple behind us asked us to put our seats up, which we did, assuming they were getting out. They remained seated. My daughter reclined her seat after a half-hour or so and again was asked to put her seat back in the upright position. I heard the woman behind us loudly whisper to her husband that they could not move when our seats were reclined. I ignored her, put my seat back, and sipped on my glass of red wine. Soon the meal service cart came through, and all seats were requested to be upright until the trays were cleared, which of course is fair enough. I tried with effort to relax myself and mentally prepare for whatever scenario lay ahead of me with my siblings as we each tried to deal with our own personal grief. The couple behind us got up to use the toilet, and after they returned, we again reclined our seats. They shook their head in disapproval at our row of three as they took their seats. Again we were asked, in a rather impatient, demanding tone, to raise our seats while they got settled back in their row. All good, but admittedly, I was growing a bit weary of their insistence for all in our row to refrain from reclining our seats.

Once we assumed them to be settled, Catherine and the girl next to her lowered their seats, and were immediately asked to *PLEASE* put their seats back up. The girl next to Catherine looked over at me and confided that she had been behind this couple at the check-in counter and witnessed a loud confrontation between them and the staff. Undeterred, I turned around and very politely informed them that we had every right to put our seats back and rest. I suggested if it was more space or legroom they wanted, they should have booked seats in business or first class. I then heard the wife say something to the effect that we were favored in that we had the bulkhead seats. I ignored her comments, put on my sleep mask and placed my seat back in an effort to get some sleep. Suddenly, my seat was being shaken violently from behind. OK . . ., that was it! No more Ms. Nice Guy.

I tore off the sleep mask, turned around in my seat and yelled, "Excuse me. What is going on? You are being incredibly rude."

"So are you," he replied.

To my utter disbelief, the moment I turned away from him, he began shaking my seat once again.

I yelled again, "That's it!" I pressed my flight attendant call light as one of the crewmembers walked by me, and I held out my hand to stop her. "Please help me. I'm being harassed. I'm being harassed," I cried.

She looked at me concerned, motioned for me to slow down, and asked me to repeat slowly to her the nature of the harassment.

"Firstly, I paid over $6000 for these two seats as my mother just died and I'm on my way back to her funeral in Texas. I need to get some rest. I'm so worn out. From the moment I sat down in this seat, my daughter, and indeed this other girl here in our row, have been forbidden and harassed by this couple behind us to put our seats upright. Just now, he has been shaking my seat like a madman to get me to put it back upright. I'm not going to stand for this outrageous behavior, not with all the money I paid to be in this seat."

She listened empathetically, and turned to the man behind me and firstly noted that both he and his wife's seats were reclined. "Sir," she began, "these women have every right to put their seats back, until the next meal service in ten hours. I can see that you and your wife have your seats in the recline position . . . ."

As she continued in her attempts to placate the offenders behind me, I placed my seat back in the recline position, put on my sleep mask, and drifted off to sleep until I was awakened with a warm face cloth and a breakfast tray. As we neared arrival, the head flight attendant approached me and bent over my seat gingerly to offer his condolences on the death in my family, and enquired if there would be any special assistance needed upon arrival to facilitate my transfer onto my next flight. All I could think of was a request to be upgraded on the next leg of my journey, which sadly was not an option.

Once in Texas, my sense of grief and loss weighed heavily upon me and all I could do was just put one foot in front of the other as my siblings gathered and paid their respects. Everything fell in to place without too much fanfare, thanks to all our efforts. Though we have had the usual sibling rivalries throughout the years, everyone willingly put these aside to lay our mother to rest. As she had many times made her burial wishes known to all of us, it was just a matter of executing them expediently and in a financially viable manner. The eldest of my brothers willingly, and without discussion, took over the helm and the rest of us basically followed instructions as to time and place.

There was a private viewing arranged for the immediate family in the mortuary, one that did not necessitate purchasing a coffin. My mother was dressed in an outfit chosen by one of my sisters and laid out on a gurney with one of her hand-knitted wool blanket throws draped over her. One by one, we all went to her and said our own very personal good-byes as a priest presided from the parish of St. Jude, the patron saint of hopeless cases, to whom my mother prayed devoutly throughout her lifetime. Catherine had written a poem to her grandmother and read this aloud with my arm around her, fighting back tears while trying to give her the emotional support she needed to get through this token of love, while my brother played the Irish flute softly in accompaniment.

The cremation was arranged for the next day, and my sister suggested we might want to be in a church during the time and so persuaded the priest to open St. Jude Catholic Church for that hour. While we sat there in our own thoughts in various pews, my younger brother's cell phone began to ring at precisely 1 p.m., the time of her cremation, and it's ring tone was a train signal, *whooo, hooo, whoo hoo* . . . . I smiled in spite of myself at the bad timing when he stood up at the front of the church, smiled and said, "That's it, guys. There she blows. That's our Mom. She's on her way to heaven."

To this day, I have never determined whether this incident was pre-meditated on his part, but it really didn't matter in the end; it seemed all very appropriate at the time. The next day kept us busy sourcing a suitable container to put her urn in for burial in Northern Ireland in a few days' time, in the grave of my oldest brother, who was buried there in 1972 after his school bus accident. A lovely, small leather trunk was agreed upon and made into a memory chest of family pictures and mementos to surround the urn, along with a Lipton tea bag in a birthday china tea cup I had bought her years ago, with a Lorna Doone shortbread cookie, and one cigarette to accompany her on her journey to heaven.

My sister's neighbors were surreptitiously dropping off casseroles for dinner and breakfast supplies all the time we were there at her house. They would slip quietly into the house and leave a bag of croissants on the kitchen counter, along with a cooked dinner for that evening. The day before the cremation, a smoker had been brought out to one of the driveways and a brisket of beef cooked away slowly all through the night in true Texas barbecue style and served for the gathering back at the house after the services. The thoughtfulness and generosity of these neighboring folk in Texas impressed me greatly.

It was not economically feasible for me to continue on to Northern Ireland for the burial, but I was comforted knowing that my mother's life was thoughtfully celebrated and honored in the personal, no-frills gathering of all her seven living children to give her a loving, heartfelt farewell.

Rest in peace, Mom . . . I miss you dearly.

Flying the Coop

WHEN I FLEW INTO WELLINGTON a few days after my mother's cremation and stared out of the window at the white-capped waters in the harbor below me, I feared I might feel displaced upon returning to New Zealand.

Catherine and I took a cab back to our apartment and I decided to go for a swim at the public indoor pool up the road to untangle the generalized cramps and aches I was feeling after the long flight back from the USA. While I was swimming, I stared out the windows at the random and swiftly moving clouds above me while the speakers blared the R.E.M. song, "Everybody Hurts, Sometimes." I knew at once I was in the right place. Comforted. I was home.

Over the next few months, my thoughts were preoccupied and in a quandary about building a house on the lot we had purchased after we first arrived to Wairarapa. As I mentioned, the house where we had been living was in an excellent location, but the floor plan was funky and the bathrooms dated so it needed too much remodeling to get it the way we would have liked, and we just didn't have the inclination to do this.

I prayed for a sign as to what to do, when to my astonishment a real estate agent's card appeared by my front door one day. The handwritten message on the back of the card indicated that he had a party interested in buying our house should we wish to sell. I thought it was just one of those ploys to get me to contact him to discuss the possibility of listing with him should we ever want to sell in the future, so I ignored it and threw the card in the trash. A few days later, I received a phone call from this agent asking if I had received his card. Again, he told me he had a very interested party, a widower who had just sold a farm and now had plenty of change clinking around in his pocket who wanted our house. I had a chat with Paul, and we thought we'd follow through to see where it might lead. The retired farmer had a viewing of the house and agreed it was exactly what he had been wanting and was willing to make an offer then and there. His first offer was decent enough, but both Paul and I had a sense that this land was worth much more, and as we had no immediate desire to move, we turned it down.

The buyer came back via the agent immediately and asked us what it would take to buy this house. We named a price which he willingly accepted and soon a contract was drawn up and signed.

This was it, my sign that we were to move and build a house on the lot we had purchased months ago and thus made the contract conditional upon the completion of our new house. At that stage, we had estimated being about eighteen months away or so. It was once again a beautiful, uncomplicated real estate transaction in New Zealand and we were very pleased with the deal we had made in less than a year of owning the house.

The pressure was on us now to get some design plans drawn and begin the whole building process, something that was completely foreign to us. I had interviewed several reputable builders in town and decided to go with the one I had originally met shortly after seeing their model show home in town. The first necessity was to discuss our budget, which would then determine the scope of work and to what ends our dreams could be financially realized in terms of design and appointment.

Months and months went by and still no design was forthcoming that seemed to reflect what we had described in our wish list. After I had threatened to terminate the contract and source another builder, a design was produced along with its projected cost, which turned out to be roughly double our budget. When the manager of the company told me the contract price, I honestly thought he was joking. But he wasn't. To further gall me, he actually shrugged his shoulders and told me what the price would be roughly converted to American dollars. American dollars! What did American dollars have to do with anything? I asked. He might as well have quoted yen to me, as we were now earning only Kiwi dollars and paying Kiwi taxes. We no longer dealt in American dollars, for God's sake!

After much deliberation and a threatened lawsuit (who says Kiwis don't sue?), I decided to go with another firm outside of town and had to begin the process all over again. Meanwhile, our purchaser was getting a bit antsy about our moving plans and began to put on the pressure, rightly so. Luckily, a house around the corner from us came on the market within our price range; we bought it just before our second Kiwi Christmas and moved yet again.

Our son, Alex, had meanwhile graduated from high school and was accepted to the University of Auckland, where he hoped to gain admission to the medical school after the required one year of pre-med health science courses.

Graduation as such from high school does not happen here as a cap and gown ceremony with fancy announcements mailed out to friends and family in hopes of financial recompense. After exams were sat, there was only a "Leaver's Ball" dinner-dance—to which parents were invited and where academic awards were presented—which marked the passage from high school, known as College here, out into the world. Alex, to his credit, walked away with the second-highest academic ranking, Proxime Accesit, in his final year.

As time neared for Alex to begin University, Paul decided to take a week off work and do a road trip with him up the hitherto unexplored west coast of the North Island, and help him get settled into his new environment. How does a mother ever feel ready to let go of one of her babes and see them start on their own life journey? No matter how mentally prepared I imagined myself to be on this day, my heart felt otherwise.

As I packed the last of his belongings into the overstuffed trunk of the car and hugged my eldest child one last time as a full-time member of our household, my heart burst with emotion and I fought back streams of tears as the car pulled out of the driveway. Where had all those years gone? From changing diapers to the first day at kindergarten, the endless homework assignments, teacher's meetings, parent volunteer committees, driving field trips, school plays, sports and puberty, it all seemed like a dream now. My eldest baby was leaving home.

Catherine, who was home from Wanganui Collegiate that weekend, put her arm around me as we walked back into the house and did her best to assure me all would be OK. She was thriving at her new school where she had started a basketball team and signed up for crew, rowing early every morning.

It would soon became clear to me that his leaving was not so much a parting but more of a stretching of love, and the elastic arms of love stretch far and wide. I had to trust, as my children trusted, that the love we shared would never change, regardless of where we were living in the world.

So, within eighteen months of arriving in New Zealand, Paul and I were effectively "empty nesters" in that we had launched Alex to University at age seventeen, and Catherine, at age sixteen, was now a full-time boarder at a school over two hours from home. It was time to get used to life being back to just Paul and me.

During Alex's first few weeks at Auckland University, he became so overwhelmed by the perceived competition to get top grades in the health science pre-med courses that he had a bit of a "melt down." He insisted that he didn't have a chance at entry into medical school in Auckland and wanted to quit and go back to university in the USA. He was living in a residence hall near the medical school and was one of the few who had a roommate assigned to his room for the year. This fellow just happened to be American, an exchange student over from U.C. Santa Barbara. This guy was in his early twenties, a junior, and was in New Zealand basically to party for a year and check out the country. In spite of saying that, he and Alex were most respectful of one another and it all worked out well for them both. He was very encouraging when Alex needed it most. The thing that really freaked Alex was that everyone in his hall had declared health sciences as a major with the hopes of getting into medical school the following year. He rang me one night and sounded defeated after only a few weeks.

"The thing is, Mom," he began, "there are so many Asians here and they never come out of their rooms. They're always studying."

"Now wait a minute," I began. "Just because they are in their rooms all the time doesn't necessarily mean they are studying the proper way, or the proper material. They also have a language barrier to overcome."

I didn't know any better. It didn't matter what I said as in his mind he had already failed and would not be eligible to achieve his goals in New Zealand. He fell into the trap of stereotyping and it was working against him.

"Hey, hey, hey . . . ," I coaxed. "Slow down. You're way ahead of yourself. What you need to do is just get through the study assignments for this week only. That's it. All you can do is your best, and then you must do the same next week. Set smaller goals for yourself."

When he scored the highest grade in the university for those first exams—99.5% in biology—he never looked back, and after his interview later that year, he was accepted into medical school for the following year. Paul's initial response surprised me. He began, "You know, Alex, you can turn it down. You don't have to pursue this path. There are plenty of other less stressful and taxing jobs and ways to make a living."

Alex remained adamant that this was his chosen path. We were, of course, elated, and Paul confided to me that if this event was the only positive outcome from our move to New Zealand, then that was a good enough validation for him.

I nodded my head in agreement. It was a great day all round.

Leaky Buildings

THE RIVALRY BETWEEN AUCKLAND AND Wellington, the two major cities of the North Island, may be compared to the same thing I experienced living in California between Los Angeles and San Francisco. It is with some amusement that stories are relayed around the country about the smugness of those living in Auckland, with their perceived lack of awareness of life south of the Bombay Hills. It was always with a sense of dread, or even apology, amongst local folk that one would mention the fact that a trip to Auckland was necessary for one thing or another.

"What's the problem with Auckland?" I asked one of my neighbors in town.

Well, for one thing, they are really up themselves, I was quickly informed. "You know," she continued, "we have a name for Aucklanders here; we call them Jafas: Just Another Fuckin' Aucklander!"

OK! As I mentioned earlier, one of our first introductions to New Zealand was via Auckland when that kind woman chauffeured us around the city and dropped us off at Domain Park. When we went back to California after a year and had a few hours to kill in Auckland, we walked around the city along Queen Street and noticed the air felt much milder in the middle of winter than in the Wairarapa valley and the average person was more smartly dressed. There were many foreign accents heard in the shops and a more cosmopolitan feel to the city than Wellington. It came as a surprise to many in our small town that our son decided to go to the University of Auckland rather than head to the South Island to Dunedin or Canterbury, where all of his classmates were going upon leaving high school. He wanted to study medicine, and after a bit of research, he decided that Auckland was a better choice for him academically; it was warmer as well.

After he was accepted to medical school, Paul and I thought it might be good idea to join the property boom in New Zealand and purchase an apartment for Alex to live for the next five years while he studied. The goal was to have a secure place for him to live with flat mates who would contribute to the mortgage payments, then sell it after he graduated to pay off his student loans. It all sounded like a very sensible idea at the time.

We were referred to a real estate agent who specialized in downtown apartments and arranged a weekend to fly up there and begin the search for something suitable and within our budget. Properties were selling briskly at that time, and one had to make offers that were fairly close to the asking price to avoid being outbid.

The agent assisting us, though young, assured us she had a handle on what the market was doing and what would be the best options for us in and around the medical school. After two offers were rejected, Paul and I flew back to Wairarapa, leaving Alex to work with the agent, aware of what the purchasing parameters and upper limits were for us. As the media was full of horror stories about the leaky building disasters in and around Auckland city, I was hyper-vigilant in my questions to the agent and had instructed Alex to always ask the same questions with regards to the integrity of the building, maintenance issues and to ask specifically if it was a leaky building, as part of the "buyer beware" policies of the time.

During the 1990s, many houses here were built using methods that included inappropriate cladding materials that did not withstand the weather conditions in New Zealand. In 1998, there was a change in the standard for timber treatment in

New Zealand, and builders were permitted to use untreated kiln-dried timber, which rots when it gets wet. The cladding, with no overhangs, along with the untreated timber has led to buildings leaking when it rains and greatly challenges the integrity of the building structure. Walls have crumbled; balconies jutting from the walls have collapsed, causing serious bodily injuries, and dangerous molds have grown in the wet timber causing increased respiratory and skin problems in residents. It is one of the most costly building scandals to date in New Zealand and the last thing any owner would want to come up against and need to correct. There are many horror stories of people losing all their savings, going bankrupt, and even committing suicide as a result of being a party to a leaky building.

A week later, Alex rang us and described what he thought was the perfect property. It was a two-bedroom townhouse, just a short walk from the Grafton Street Bridge and well appointed, with a view of the Auckland Sky Tower from the upper-floor bedroom. The price was at the higher end of what we had hoped to spend but our bank had no problem loaning us the full amount. So, an offer was made and accepted, and the contract given to a local solicitor in town to review before we signed it to make it binding. I confirmed with the agent that the building was sound, had no maintenance issues and was not one of those— God forbid—leaky buildings, to which she replied that all was good, not to worry, even going as far as to suggest I was being a bit paranoid. Later, Alex also verified that he had asked the same questions when he went back to view the property with the agent and the seller. Yes, he told me, they assured him there were no problems.

All good . . . .

The contract became unconditional, but I still wanted to read the body corporate minutes before we settled and closed the deal, as that would have had any up-to-date issues that may need to be addressed immediately. Looking back in hindsight,

I should have insisted upon reading them before the contract became unconditional, but again I believed I was dealing with professionals. The agent assured me she would e-mail them as an attachment and that it was our solicitor's job to review them as part of the conveyance. This I confirmed with the solicitor and was duly assured he would inform me if there was any need for concern. So, I relaxed and enjoyed the company of my good friends Kim and Marianne visiting from Long Beach, California while these professionals were handling the details. Sadly, I didn't heed Kim's advice as a successful real estate broker to fly up to Auckland and inspect the building myself. I had become a bit too complacent in my newly expanded role as property investor.

The day we became the legal owners and the key was handed over to Alex, he called me to say that he had met the next-door neighbors, who asked him if he was aware of the south wall having maintenance issues. I assured him that whatever it was, it could not be that serious as we had asked all the right questions and the building had been verbally verified by both the agent and the seller as being sound and in good condition.

In the meantime, I had contacted a friend of mine who was in interior design to help Alex buy some furniture and other essentials to get him moved in as soon as possible, and I arranged to fly up that first weekend after we had become the owners to help him get settled. It was with great excitement that I packed a duvet set, sheets, towels, blender, sandwich toaster and a bottle of champagne into my suitcases and looked forward to the weekend ahead celebrating Alex's new home for the next few years.

The taxi dropped me off in front of the building, and I let myself in the front door dragging the two heavy suitcases behind me. Overall, my first impression was very favorable and the row of terraced townhouses in the middle of the city reminded me again a bit of Paddington, Sydney. Obviously, I have very good memories of my stay there upon arrival "down under." As I dragged one suitcase up the stairs to our flat, I was warmly greeted by a few of the owners coming down the stairs.

"Hello! You must be the new owner? We live next door," Mike said, and introduced me to his partner standing next to him, Scott.

"Actually, my husband and I bought it for our son who is in medical school at the University of Auckland. I'm just up for the weekend to help him move in. Looks like a great spot and a wonderful location too!" I said, smiling.

There was a few seconds of silence as the other owners looked at one another with some hesitation before speaking. "Now, you do know about the south wall, don't you?" Mike began.

"No, only that Alex just told me early this week that he heard there were some maintenance issues?

"Well, you might say that. Actually, there are some rather serious maintenance issues," Scott added.

I dropped my suitcase beside me and looked directly at him. "What do you mean, serious maintenance issues? Don't tell me this is a leaky building?" I begged.

Mike covered his mouth for a second and turned to his partner and made a shocked face.

"Oh my God! She doesn't know. I had a feeling they weren't told. And that wretch. She swore to us that she had told you," Mike continued.

"Told me what?"

"This is showing signs of being a leaky building."

My stomach started churning and my eyes immediately welled up with tears. Mike lifted my suitcase and escorted me to our new townhouse, and opened the door for me, which led to the front door via a courtyard. He then offered to make me a cup of tea at his place. After the second suitcase was brought in, Alex appeared in the courtyard, and his face dropped once he saw me crying.

"Mom, what's the matter? Don't you like it?"

"Oh, honey." I began. "We bought into a leaky building."

"Oh no!" he gasped.

When Paul called me later that day to ask how it was going, and was Alex happy with it all, I could not bring myself to tell him over the phone of our impending financial disaster. When I arrived back at our house in Wairarapa, I fixed us some martinis and guardedly broke the news to him. I had no idea how he would react, but there is a reason why we are still married after thirty-odd years. He just looked at me, shook his head and said, "Ah hell. It's only money. We'll manage."

Am I married to a saint or what?

Well, after two years as plaintiffs in a costly legal battle against the agent, seller and the solicitor handling the escrow, we got it all sorted and settled to a somewhat satisfactory degree, even though we had to break into most of our U.S. retirement funds to do so. Indeed, we have had more dealings with solicitors and legal proceedings here in New Zealand since arriving than we've ever had in the USA, and we herald from one of the most litigious states in the nation and in the world. It galls me to no end that folk here still insist that New Zealanders do not sue. Certainly not true in my own personal and costly experience.

This fiasco could have easily derailed my marriage and made us bitter and resentful in the face of burning through so much money, but I firmly believe it is not what is thrown at us but how we deal with it that makes or breaks us as people. I witnessed my own father lose everything in a disastrous business venture back in Ireland and he never got over it.

To be fair, I was a bit sloppy in this real estate transaction in that although I asked all the right questions to the right people and did my due diligence as they say here, I neglected to do what I have done in the past, and that is to have a chat with one of the neighbors about the building, area, etc. They would have been more than happy to divulge the latest findings detailed in the minutes from the last body corporate meeting, which my solicitor failed to read. There's no doubt he is more alert in his legal responsibilities as they relate to real estate transactions after the lessons learned from my case.

The building is now all re-clad and looking fantastic. In the end, we were truly fortunate in our leaky building saga as every owner came forth with his or her allocated share of funds to do the extensive re-cladding and upgrading of the building as was decided and voted upon by the body corporate. Unfortunately, new cases of leaky buildings are popping up in the newspaper daily with an alarming regularity and there remain thousands of not-so-happy endings in this disgraceful national building scandal.

Visitors and Road Rage

WHEN WE LEFT CALIFORNIA, THERE were many promises from friends and family of visits to come to our new home as soon as we got settled. The first guest of honor was one of my dearest and oldest friends, Carol. She swore she was not going to let me out of her clutches that easily. True to her word, she flew over from Portland only four months after we moved, in early November 2004, with a list of sights to visit from her extensive research on my area and Wharekauhau Estate was high on her list. I took the train down to Wellington, then a taxi to the airport to meet her upon arrival, as I was not yet confident to drive alone over the winding Rimutaka hill pass.

As we walked around the city, we could not help but feel the infectious excitement and anticipation in the air, and noticed the well-dressed downtown professionals lining up in long queues outside New Zealand betting shops, called T.A.B.s here. After a few inquiries, we were told that this was Melbourne Cup day, "the race that stops a nation."

Dating back to 1861, it is run every year in Victoria on the first Tuesday of November. While it is a national holiday in Australia, some of the larger cities of New Zealand call it a day after lunch, then join the punters in the city sports bars to share in the excitement and bet on a winning horse. Carol and I decided to make a bet on a horse that took our fancy, and she wound up winning over $100, which was quickly spent on wine at the bar at the Intercontinental Hotel, where I had booked us a room for the night. I hadn't realized that "The Cup" was only one race . . . and imagined myself to be settled in for the evening when it was actually run and over in less than a few minutes.

We weren't sitting too long with our wine in hand when a conversation began between chatty Carol and a gentlemen sitting at the next table. Upon some friendly coaxing, we learned he was a government official visiting from Canada, which is not surprising as Wellington is the capital and seat of government. After introductions and a few pleasantries were exchanged, the conversation shifted to New Zealand idioms and manners when I mentioned that I had trouble with the phrase "Sweet as," commonly used here, explaining that I was always left hanging waiting to hear the sentence finished. The man gave me a rather curious look when I asked him if he agreed with me.

"I don't know what you mean," he answered.

"Haven't you heard them say 'sweet as' here?" I asked.

"Ohhh . . . . Forgive me, but I thought you were saying, Sweet *Ass.*" A misunderstanding that brought on many laughs and another round of drinks on him. That afternoon proved for Carol to be a positive introduction to the Kiwi lifestyle I was learning to love.

Arriving back to Wairarapa, I took Carol to our local veggie stand to buy some vegetables for dinner, as over the years she ate less and less meat and was now a vegetarian bordering on vegan. And gluten intolerant as well. A very easy guest indeed— NOT. I was amused to find her analyzing the New Zealand yams, which she decided reminded her of grubs, and wondering if a tamarillo was a fruit or a vegetable. I was happy to inform her that I had done some research on tamarillos and learned that they were once known as "tomate de arbol," the lost foods of the Incas, which have all but disappeared from their natural habitat. They are a relative of the tomato, eggplant and capsicum pepper, native to Central and South America and introduced to New Zealand in the late 1800s. Soon thereafter, an Auckland nurseryman developed the red ones from South America from seed. This clever New Zealander changed its name from tree tomato to tamarillo to avoid confusion with the common garden tomato, in the same vein that Chinese gooseberry was changed and are now known as Kiwi fruit to increase its popularity in the commercial markets. By combining a Māori word, tama, which implies leadership in Māori language, along with the Spanish word amarillo, meaning yellow—as originally only yellow ones were imported from Asia—the name tamarillo was born.

Tamarillos have become a traditional Kiwi food icon. During World War II, demand for tamarillos grew as the supply for other fruits high in Vitamin C was severely restricted. They can be used a variety of ways including in chutneys, sauces and relishes. I even made a tamarillo martini once as a novel treat for recent guests.

Carol was here only a few days when the 2004 USA presidential election took place and she was obsessed with watching live coverage as the votes were tallied, hoping desperately that George W. Bush would not be re-elected for a second term. She pined for the country to be led by the democratic candidate, John Kerry. Thinking she was sitting in the comfort of her Portland living room, she flicked through our measly three channels and became quickly frustrated in her attempts to find any coverage of the election outside the normally televised news hours.

"What kind of country is this? The first thing on the news is the results of some rugby game? Where is Fox or CNN news?" she wailed, holding the television remote up in the air.

It took her a while to comprehend that we did not have the SKY satellite dish that was needed to have access to these channels, and that I had no intention of getting this service while we lived in the rental house.

An Irish couple from Dublin had warned me shortly before leaving California about the substandard news reporting in my newly adopted country. They had just come from New Zealand via Fiji when I met them at the restaurant at the trendy Mission Inn in Carmel. When I told them we were planning to move to New Zealand in a few months' time, they looked at me in utter bewilderment. Before this, all reactions to our move had been one of good-natured envy, a longing to live in Hobbit-land.

"Why in heavens would you ever even consider living there? Have you ever watched the evening news in New Zealand? They're so insular, so backward. There are about fifty-five minutes of local news and a grand total of only five minutes for global affairs. No, no. Definitely not the place for me. Too removed."

To be fair, there are many headlines, both in the national newspapers and our local weekly that provoke laughs from me to this day. Recent news has included the unrest in Syria, a global refugee crisis, rebellions in Greece and Spain about financial austerity measures imposed on them by Germany, and a very controversial U.S. presidential election. And what do I read on the front page of the *Dominion Post*? The headline: "Storeman viewed porn to take his mind off demanding work."

What? What kind of demanding work? He was a storeman at a bathroom supply retail store, for God's sake. Let's talk about real demanding work!

Meanwhile, Carol was visibly growing more and more agitated. "How can you live like this? So out of touch with the world?" she asked me.

I assured her that I was as informed on world affairs as I wanted or needed to be and no matter what, the world would go on as it always does, as it always has whether I kept abreast of events or not. Her sense of impatience placed a strain on the rest of our short time together. Tensions between us were not helped by the fact that she began drinking her chilled wine around 4 p.m.-ish was asleep close to 7 p.m. most evenings, even before dinner was served. Yet, she whined about not seeing the Southern Cross in the sky, which necessitated her staying awake till dark. Having slept most of the evening and night, she would then waken before sunrise close to 5 a.m., go for her thirty- to forty-minute jog, and be raring to get going by 8 a.m. I seemingly could not do anything right in her eyes, and sadly had to accept that our twenty-five year plus friendship was now being put to the test. I had very literally moved on.

We said our farewells in Napier, where we spent the weekend touring the Hawkes Bay area, and the Gannet bird colony at Cape Kidnappers. Carol had made plans to do a tour around Auckland and the Bay of Islands, and I was heading back to Wairarapa alone in my car. It was my first long-distance drive since I had arrived, but any misgivings I had on the three-hour drive home quickly vanished as I hummed along happily on totally empty roads. I kept repeating to myself, Oh my God . . . I'm on a major highway and there's no traffic, no cars! Yeah! I was ecstatic to have had seen only a few cars and trucks the entire drive home, and again knew I was in the right place in my life.

After Carol left for home, we had four more years of President Bush to contend with and more and more anti-American sentiment in the air. The war in Iraq was escalating, as was the war in Afghanistan and the media in New Zealand would have one believe that the Americans were warmongers, especially to blame for all this unrest in the world. It was only the people who had traveled to the USA who held a more global view of world affairs. It surprised me when a nurse from the hospital told me she was shocked to discover that Americans were "really nice people." and "very generous" when she had recently visited relatives in Chicago and San Francisco.

Admittedly, I missed the American exuberance and generosity of spirit and felt an acute pang in my heart. There was never any real sense of celebration amongst the folk I met in my new social arena. New Zealanders are, in my experience, too reserved and self-conscious to want to stick out too much, part of the "Tall Poppy" notion they hold that no one should live or behave in an over the top, flamboyant manner.

Holiday celebrations like Halloween or New Year's Eve are very subdued, if celebrated at all. Again, it is still very strange for me to fill my vases with iris and tulips in October, rather than putting pumpkins outside my front door and bowls of decorative Native American squash on my dining table.

Our next American visitor was Catherine's best friend, Selina, who came out alone for two weeks over her Christmas holidays. We were in our new home then, and this was to be our first Christmas in New Zealand. Catherine and I set about devising a bit of a tour to make the most of her friend's time on holiday. It was decided we should spend the first night at our apartment in Wellington and go see a Christmas pantomime, Cinderella, which was playing at one of the theaters in the city. I was looking forward to getting some Christmas spirit in the city with all the shops. To my dismay, it was just like any other weekend with no effort to dress the shop windows in Christmas-themed fare. It was business as usual with shopping hours closing at 6 p.m. on the Saturday before Christmas. My only hope was that Selina would be more interested in seeing a bit of New Zealand rather than celebrating Christmas in an American tradition.

That year, we were invited to choose a tree from our friend's nearby farm and set about looking through the remainder of unopened boxes for whatever Christmas decorations and items I managed to hold onto before the move. As I mentioned previously, upon Paul's advice, I had given away many decorations to our former housekeeper, but soon contented myself with the notion that less is more. The finished decorated tree brought to mind a Charlie Brown-type of affair, but the lights twinkled merrily and there were plenty of wrapped presents under the tree. The warm weather was upon us and we felt it was rather like San Diego at this time of the year. Plump, ripe strawberries were in season and being sold in shops everywhere in town and from produce stands along the main roads. And Lindauer Special Reserve sparkling wine, "Bubbles," my personal favorite here, was selling for half-price at most markets. What more could one want?

My South African friend who had dragged me along to my first morning tea, Taoni, kindly invited us to her house for a Christmas Eve dinner, and asked that we bring a vegetable side dish to share for the table. After 5 p.m. Mass in town, which was surprisingly well-attended, we headed over to our friend's house for the evening, where two beautifully set tables awaited us, along with a bag of wrapped gifts to be shared and fought over in a Lucky Dip. It was all a very relaxed affair and comforting in the sense that we felt part of an extended family that year.

After Christmas, we had planned a "girl's trip" with another American woman and her daughter who had recently arrived in Wairarapa, to head up the North Island and do the popular tourist sights and activities for our guest. It was the first time since our camping trip that we had driven through the sulfur-filled air of Rotorua, bathed in the hot pools of the Polynesian Spa, toured the Waitomo caves, and stopped off at Taupo for the night to the delight of the girls. We took a boat ride across the lake and I was reminded that my son had told me rumors about the "bush" Māori living in the hills who often rattled the folk who freedom camped around the lake, as this was their land after all. I doubted there were eyes looking at us now from the "bush" as I scanned the hills and passed it off as a joke on tourists. When we pulled up beside the jetty, there were a couple of strapping, young Māori lads who were gleefully jumping and doing cannonballs off the jetty into the frosty lake water, splashing the obviously delighted Asian tourists who were frantically clicking their cameras from an amphibious duck boat docked in front of us.

As I passed one of the boys, I remarked, "Wow! You boys are brave to be jumping into that cold water."

To which he strutted and replied, "We're MÃORI," his chest forward and pulling his shoulders backwards with a sense of pride and defiance.

I thought better than to ask if he was one of the "bush" Māori folk.

Our next stop was Gisborne on the East Cape and the first city in the world to greet the sun of a new day. Karen had wanted to go to the beach where the movie *Whale Rider* had been filmed, and it was with some effort I got some information on the area from the local tourist center. I was duly informed that it might prove a bit of a challenge getting access to the beach in the small settlement Whangara, north of Gisborne, if I didn't know a local who was connected to the area. Apparently, tourists inundated Whangara after the film and showed no regard for Māori history and tradition, along with no respect for the sanctity of the marae there. A person at the Gisborne tourist office happily gave me a phone number of a gentleman in the settlement that would welcome us to the area.

Well, several determined attempts to reach this gentleman left me generally put off by his rather gruff manner and arrogance. I was genuinely interested in learning some pertinent history about the settlement along with the role of the marae in the community only to be answered with an air of suspicion and dismissal. The final insult happened when he directed the conversation to "business," informing me that he charged $50 an hour for his services, which included his time opening the marae, walking along the beach and "a bit of history," though he advised that it would not be possible to give an account of 2000 years of Māori history of the area in just one hour.

"$50 an hour?" I confirmed.

"Yes. $50 an hour. Per person."

Well I don't think so! This quote rather shocked me, to be honest, as I was informed by the tourist office that if indeed there were a cost, it would most likely be a Koha donation; a Māori way of expressing gratitude and can be in the form of a physical gift, like money, food or a bottle of fancy wine. Ah well, I was promised by a local friend up in the area that she would take me there another time. No worries. And fair enough that the villagers want their privacy and peace.

New Zealand in summer is absolutely humming with excitement and movement. During the few days leading up to Christmas, the roads are clogged with folk in cars packed to the rafters with holiday items, all heading to their seaside homes or baches. The holiday traffic picks up again the day after 26 December, Boxing Day. I was warned to make reservations everywhere as this was one of the most popular times for natives and tourists alike to be exploring around the country, in contrast to my experience back in San Diego where it seemed everyone stayed close to home at Christmas time.

The roads were indeed busy, and it was fun to see so many cars at one time, towing boats, motorbikes, canoes, and all types of toys along for their enjoyment. Every time someone passed us on the road, I would make a point of saying, "Kiwis on the move . . ." and found this all very entertaining until we were forced to follow the very car who had just passed us and then refused to keep up with the posted speed of 100 kilometers per hour.

"What the heck is going on here?" I asked my friend Karen. This happened nearly every time we were on a stretch of road with a passing lane and it was the same scenario. Firstly, the car behind us would tailgate and flash the lights for us to let them pass. OK, no problem there as we were not in a rush. Then the car would overtake us and immediately reduce its speed, forcing us to lag behind until the next opportunity to pass in the road was announced. As soon as our car would gather enough speed and exit to the passing lane, the car in front would speed up again and prevent our car from getting ahead, a ridiculous cat and mouse game.

Though it remains infuriating to this day, I have come to accept it as inevitable, in the same manner I tolerate the exaggerated responses to an incident where the other driver perceives he has been cut off or dismissed. Though this is clearly a blanket statement, Kiwis tend to lose all points for graciousness once they get behind the wheel of a car. It's as if any deep-seated aggressions are free to be released on the road.

I have heard from two American friends that they were followed and harassed on the road after entering a roundabout too early and perceived as "cutting" off the other car. One was tailgated from the next town back into Wairarapa by an angry man with two young children in his car. The other was a woman who was followed by a man for over forty minutes; he insisted she had cut him off near her daughter's school. Not too far from her house in the country, she spotted a police car behind her with flashing lights and stopped, only to be told that he had received a call giving her license plate and stating that she was noted to be driving recklessly.

Once while my daughter was driving my car in Palmerston North displaying her red learner "L" placard highly visible from both the front and back windows, she realized she was in the wrong turning lane and would have to drive around the entire block to make the turn. I was sitting beside her in the passenger seat and asked her to roll down the window so I could motion to the lady in the Land Rover beside me to do the same. I reached over Catherine, looked at the elder lady and asked her if she would please mind if we moved ahead of her into her lane to make the right-hand turn at the traffic light.

"Certainly not," she began, shaking her head in the negative and giving me this look of utter abhorrence. "You'll simply have to wait your turn. Like the rest of us."

I opened my mouth in shock, and to my surprise, both Catherine and I said in unison, "I don't believe this!" and I gave her . . . yes, the finger!! Just couldn't help myself.

I ran this scene by the ladies in my morning tea group to get some support and most thought this was not atypical behavior. "She was right. No way would I have let you in," one quickly informed me.

Another agreed, "What? And then me miss the light because you weren't paying attention in the first place. Sorry, missus, but you were in the wrong."

Who's to know where all that lovely Kiwi charm and congeniality disappears to when a native gets behind the wheel of a car? It's as if the car becomes a safe haven to vent all the pent-up rage and frustrations of the day with some anonymity and lack of culpability. Obviously, no one has heard about the notion of driving with aloha, as they say in Hawaii. Or with native *Aroha*.

Knowing this about Kiwi drivers, I try to put extra effort into using common courtesy whenever I can on local roads here and try to allow a car to turn in when it can and respond with a smile if someone cuts me off on the roundabout. I take delight when sometimes I get a nod of appreciation for my thoughtful efforts. People are people no matter where we go and everyone just wants to be treated with a little thoughtfulness and kindness. There have been occasions recently when a car has stopped to permit me to enter traffic, or cross over the road, or not race me to the petrol pumps. Yep, wonders never cease. It's simply not worth getting angry or upset over such trivial matters.

Back to summers in New Zealand . . . how this country pulses with outdoor activity. As I mentioned before, cars are packed to capacity and roads are jammed with holiday makers heading to their lake or coastal baches; campgrounds are filled and vineyards become the venues for top-performing acts and concerts. New Zealanders often cringe when overseas people refer to their country as "quaint" or it being about twenty years behind the USA. And they are certainly correct; it is not. Quaint is not necessarily a disparaging or offensive description of this country in my mind. It refers to a sense of community and hospitality.

Nevertheless I am reminded of my summers as a child back in the 1960s on the East Coast of the USA. It is all go, go, go with regards to barbecues, picnics, tramps in the hills, surfing and daylight that lasts until close to 10 p.m. This is truly a season to be fully appreciated, the happiest and most relaxed time of the year, when all those long, drab nights and rains of winter become a distant memory. The entire country here switches gears into holiday mode, an infectious feeling no one can escape. Just try to find a tradesman from Christmas until late January. It's as if the country just shuts down and waits for the New Year to begin, then working life is suspended for a few weeks to enjoy family and friends doing what Kiwis do best in their own backyards . . . barbecues and any activity outdoors.

Having experienced several winters here, I can accept the reasons proffered why they seem so long. It's simply due to the fact there are no holidays here to break up this season as there are in the USA, e.g. Halloween, Thanksgiving, Christmas, New Year's and Valentine's Day. The endless cold, damp and grey days, punctured too infrequently for me with glorious clear blue skies, with no celebrations to plan for and anticipate along the way make the winter feel like it is going on and on until Labor Day weekend arrives at the end of October.

New Zealand is the first country in the world to greet the sunrise of the New Year and it is with an ache in my heart that it is celebrated here with little or no fanfare. There is no Dick Clark celebrity figure to tune in to and share the countdown as the Big Apple is dropped down in Times Square in New York. I have to wait close to twenty hours before I can call friends at midnight overseas to wish them a Happy New Year. It's just not the same. It was going to be tough to beat that first New Year's we spent on the yacht in Sydney Harbor, but I had hoped by sharing it with friends in Wellington, there might be some fanfare to celebrate my first New Zealand New Year's Eve. Paul was "on call" that New Year's holiday, and as Catherine had her friend visiting from California, I thought there would be more of a buzz about Wellington city. Friends of mine had also invited me to dinner at a restaurant near our apartment, knowing that I would be without Paul for the night.

The first thing immediately apparent upon arriving in Wellington was that there were plenty of parking spaces and hardly any cars on the road with very few pedestrians walking the streets. It was rather like a ghost town compared to the usual hustle and bustle I would encounter as I drove past the Westpac sports stadium. Where had everyone gone, I wondered. To the beach, of course! Most of the permanent residents had vacated the city, leaving only tourists to fill the galleries and cafés. Nevertheless, I figured there would be more going on there than in Wairarapa and I looked forward to dressing up and going to the White House restaurant, one of the high-end dining destinations in Wellington. Not! The tables were set as if it were any other day, with nothing to denote the atmosphere of New Year's Eve, at least not an American-style New Year's Eve. I had hoped for some festive atmosphere in the way of balloons and silver and black decorations, but this was not the case. I kept my eye on my watch, hoping there may be some mention from the staff or my new friends of the approaching new year by way of a countdown, but again I was disappointed.

We left the restaurant about fifteen minutes before midnight, after quite a satisfying meal with good local wine and entertaining banter, and yet, I was just not right. I was distracted by the time ticking away and that soon a new year would be upon us with no fanfare or recognition. As it neared midnight, I looked at my friends and told them there was no way I could not do my own countdown, and so with a restrained enthusiasm, I began: "10, 9, 8, 7, . . . Happy New Year!" I called out.

My friends looked at me somewhat apologetically, and then we hugged and went on our own different ways home to start the year. Ever since that experience, I have determined to always have a countdown with the same sense of excitement I have felt all my life as it nears midnight, and kiss my husband tenderly and very gratefully after screeching "Happy New Year!" Then, instead of ringing friends back in the USA, I now ring my own children, out on the town in some part of New Zealand, and shout into the receiver, "Happy New Year!!"

Sweet as . . . .

Sometime during our first year here in 2005, a fellow American living in Wairarapa relayed to me that *Time* magazine did a survey on happiness amongst certain groups of people and it was Americans who ranked the highest overall in most areas. That has sadly since changed with the current American politics. I must confess that I've not felt a sense of contentment or happiness on my last few trips back to the USA. After the housing bubble burst and with the aftermath of the sub-prime mortgage and banking crisis, I tend to get involuntarily wrapped up in the resentment, fear and unhappiness when I am there visiting friends back in California.

I think it's currently Denmark and Scandinavia in general that rank the highest on the global happiness scale. In another study, Americans came out tops for best husband qualities and Australia ranked amongst the lowest!

Aside from the pristine, smog-free air that hits me when I deplane in Auckland, it's the unhurried and relaxed pace of the everyday lifestyle that impresses and welcomes me back here the most. Tucked away as it is at the bottom of the world, it is this geographic quirk of fate that isolates New Zealand from many of the modern-day hassles of traffic, overcrowding and competition for the best that life has to offer in terms of natural beauty. There is no healthcare crisis as such here, and no one seems to be obsessed with the price of prescription medications or growing old as they are in the USA. Everyday life is just a lot less hassle in this country; on a warm sunny day in Wellington, the café tables overflow onto the sidewalks, layers of clothing are peeled back and one cannot help but think that all seems well with the world.

At least, in *MY* world . . . .

Torn Between Two Continents

A FEW MONTHS AFTER MY mother passed away, I received a phone call from the administrator at the assisted-care residential facility where my father had been living when I left San Diego, to inform me that his rent was over $40,000 in arrears. What was I going to do about it?

How in God's name could this have happened? I wondered, as I had had him set up on direct debit from his bank account directly to his facility to pay all his expenses with more than adequate funds in his account? Our bank statement was still showing our top-up deductions paid directly to his facility. Something was just not add-ing up.

When I went to visit him on our first trip back to California after a year here in New Zealand, all seemed well and he was in good form, albeit lonely. He was thrilled to see us all again and asked about when he might come to join us in New Zealand, as I had hoped to do once we got settled. As he was restless, I bought him a round-trip ticket on the Amtrak train from San Diego so he could go spend two weeks over Thanksgiving holidays with my younger brother in the San Francisco area and visit my sister in Marin County as well.

After many phone calls back and forth across the Pacific, I finally learned that my father had closed his existing bank account due to fears he was being robbed and opened a new account with a different bank. In doing this, he neglected to authorize a direct debit to his facility as I had done for him, When he received his bank statements, he understood he had all this extra money to spend on whatever whim took his fancy. He had a particular thing for television infomercials and believed every product being promoted was designed specifically for him in mind. And so he ordered and ordered, until his room looked like a mini K-mart department store. Why the attendants at the facility did not question this behavior sooner, or indeed notice that his rent was not being paid until months on down the road infuriated me. He was clearly showing the first signs of an organic brain syndrome, early dementia.

My father began insisting he wanted to go back to live in Ireland, near his family there. There was no use reminding him that he had tried that several times in the past, most recently with his second wife, and still could not settle himself there. He was inherently a restless person at the best of times. I contacted each of my six siblings living in the USA and no one made any useful suggestions or offers of any assistance to help with his predicament. Feeling desperate, I started making phone calls to relatives in Ireland to help get him placed in an independent living center. All those efforts proved abortive and frustrating. In the end, it became evident that I would have to be there in Ireland with him to get anything done.

In the meantime, I contacted the immigration services here in New Zealand to explore the options of bringing my father over here to live out his days. As we were not yet citizens, this was not advisable. I was informed that as I had more siblings residing in the USA than in New Zealand, I could not truthfully declare that I was his only child alive responsible for his care. Suffice it to say I passed many tormented months trying to get him settled into another decent facility with little luck.

In the end, Paul paid the exorbitant outstanding balance to the facility with our own money, only to be informed that my father was being evicted from his wonderful situation. He was placed in a nursing home closer to downtown San Diego before I could even react. It was a dump, as most of them are, filled with lost and forgotten souls roaming the corridors, tied into wheelchairs or left sitting, eyes glazed in front of the television. Luckily, he didn't last too long in that environment and died soon after placement, from what I believe to have been loneliness and sheer lack of hope.

It haunts me to this day.

Shortly before he died, I visited him in the hospital on my way back from a cousin's reunion in Northern Ireland. Although it had been only a few months since I had last seen him, he barely resembled himself, gaunt as he lay wrapped with blankets in the bed. My heart cried out for him, and I felt so helpless as he stared with great surprise at me. He seemed resigned to accept his pending fate and wanted me to verify with him the plans we had discussed in his will before I moved. I assured him all his wishes would be respected and that he would be laid to rest alongside other close relatives back in our parish cemetery in County Tyrone, Northern Ireland.

Four weeks later, he drew his last breath at the same hospital in San Diego where Catherine had been born. I contacted his brother in Ireland and arrangements were made to have his body cremated in San Diego, then brought back to Northern Ireland for a funeral mass and burial. I placed some stones I had carried with me to put in his grave, and also on my mother's grave so they would have a piece of New Zealand in the soil with them. He now rests on a hill a few rows away from my mother, whom he had divorced over twenty years ago, overlooking the house where we lived in Trillick during the 1970s. His epitaph echoes the words of William Wordsworth's "Ode to Immortality," "Though nothing can bring back the hour of Splendour in the grass . . ."

May he rest in peace.

Having lost both my parents within a few years of moving here, it made me address my own mortality a bit more immediately, and what my dying wishes might be in light of their recent deaths. After burying my father and perusing the headstones of close family members in the same graveyard, including my mother buried in the grave of my eldest brother, I decided that I too would like to be buried in this cemetery.

If anything, it would give my children good cause to visit Ireland and maintain a connection with their roots. It is still very much an Irish custom to visit the graves after Mass on a Sunday, and every so often, a day is put aside for a grave tidy-up. I agree with my father's idea that when one is visiting another family grave and walks by his grave, they might stop and remember time spent in his company or family stories of him and then offer a wee prayer for him. Hopefully the same will happen for me as well. My husband has since decided that he might as well be buried where I am too.

When asked where is "home" for me, I am often hesitant to answer as I have lived and made a home in many places over my fifty-eight years. Home is now New Zealand, and though we are culturally and still proudly American, I am tied to Ireland, my spiritual home, and Paul is tied to me, and that's where our weary cremated remains will rest someday, in Northern Ireland, which will be my final home.

Life Goes on in Rural New Zealand

I'T'S ONLY PAUL AND I now, and Catherine's delightful little poodle Simba, living in the home we designed and built a few kilometers outside the town of Wairarapa, true "empty nesters." We are fortunate in that we can plan to escape part of winter here during the month of July and visit family and friends back in California. They are always excited to introduce us as "our friends from New Zealand." It is almost immediate the response of surprise and intrigue from strangers when we tell them we live in New Zealand. They question us about the lifestyle and work environment, the healthcare system and education. *How did you manage that?* Their eyes almost glaze over in wonder and desire. I am quick to assure them that New Zealand is not some fantasy paradise on earth, but that it ticks a lot of boxes for us.

When I am back amongst my old friends and neighborhood in San Diego, I am reminded of how wonderful it all was to live there and raise our children, but our move to New Zealand has afforded us so many more wonderful life experiences and rewarding new friendships. The best thing about deplaning in Auckland after the long international flight from California is walking the green line over to the Domestic Terminal to connect to our next short flight to Wellington. The almost giddy joy I feel filling my nostrils with fresh New Zealand air and scanning the sky and cloud cover, or lack of it, above me never fails to surprise me. I am at once happy and grateful to be almost home safely.

Alex graduated from Auckland medical school over five years ago and is training long hours to be an orthopedic surgeon. He has successfully passed all parts of the U.S. medical licensing exam and scored high enough to be a competitive applicant to any training program there, but has decided to do his training in New Zealand. As he often tells Paul and me, for an outdoor enthusiast like him, New Zealand covers all the bases.

He truly enjoys practicing medicine along with his enviable lifestyle in New Zealand surfing, tramping, fishing and socializing with friends in the Bay of Plenty, where his lovely wife was raised. I couldn't have chosen a better or more loving daughter-in-law or life partner for my son. Last year they gave birth to our beautiful granddaughter, Greer, whom I call GG for Gorgeous Greer, and I can never get enough time holding and cuddling her. The best news recently is that he's taking a post soon at Wellington Hospital, which will be much closer to us. Did someone say Sunday lunches? I'm so looking forward to seeing him and his family more often.

Catherine graduated from Victoria University in Wellington a few years ago with a business degree in International Commerce and Marketing and is now living and working in Sydney. She needed to "flap her wings a little" and felt that Wellington and New Zealand in general was just a tad too small for her. I'm happy that she chose to live just *across the ditch* as it is only a three-hour or so flight to Sydney. With the many discounted airfares offered throughout the year, I can go visit her and make a long weekend out of the trip. There could be a lot worse cities to visit! She has made Sydney her home now and is very involved in sailing and is a member in her own right at the CYCA Yacht Club at Rushcutters Bay. Presently she's working towards getting her skipper and yachtsman credentials. I'm indeed blessed and so lucky to have both children living in very desirable spots that provide an occasional needed respite from Wairarapa when a bit more stimulation is required.

And my dear patient husband, Dr. Paul? He is still practicing as a rural general surgeon at Wairarapa Hospital and continues to enjoy working unencumbered by the many hassles of American-styled medicine. He is well liked and regarded amongst his peers and patients alike. He seems as happy as he can be and is grateful. Our marriage remains strong through the stressful trials and tribulations of general life, raising teenagers, moving to another part of the world and adapting to new social mores and norms and financial glitches. In general, I would have to say the move greatly strengthened our family unit, as with no friends or family support in this part of the world, we had only each other to depend upon, for better or for worse during those first few years in New Zealand. I tease Paul that since we've moved here he is truly my best friend.

Over the past few years, I realized my dream of starting a business, Let's Do Lunch, and host hands-on cooking classes in my home, which proves very challenging and satisfying, but alas not very lucrative. After my daughter moved from Wellington, I lost my faithful assistant and "kitchen bitch," as she jokingly referred to herself, and it became more work than I could physically handle. I do miss the fun of introducing guests to new recipes and the process of cooking a meal together and perhaps will take it up once again in the future. During that time, I joined the world of bloggers on Wordpress.com with a blog called *Sheepless in New Zealand*, which describes personal takes on daily life in rural New Zealand along with a daily recipe.

This morning as I brushed my teeth, I saw in the mirror cows quietly grazing behind me on the other side of the fence up the hill from our house, and heard sheep bleating anxiously from some other nearby paddock. The only traffic outside is the twice-daily queue of dairy cattle across the river moving stoically towards the milking shed. The summer vegetable garden is growing a variety of lettuces, chili peppers, zucchinis, tomatillos, and many varieties of heirloom tomatoes and herbs. The sky is clear, the distant Tararua Mountains well defined and the Ruamahanga River is trickling down its rocky course through the valley below our house. The hills have lost their velvety verdant hues and are now burnt amber with the abundant sunshine at this time of year and lack of rainfall, reminiscent of Northern California.

I've grown accustomed to viewing the Southern Cross in the dark uncluttered night sky rather than the Big Dipper, and seeing Orion's Belt in the summer month of January, and Scorpio in the winter month of July. I often stare in awe at the thick blanket of Milky Way stars in the dark skies above our home in Wairarapa, unpolluted by the electric beams pouring from homes, office building, and street lights. According to a recent article in *Time* magazine, the light pollution in the USA has become so bad that it is estimated that eight out of ten children born today will never encounter a sky dark enough for them to see the Milky Way. How sad is that; to go through one's life and never see a starry, starry night?

I surprise myself when I involuntarily slip into the role of New Zealand ambassador when I am overseas, educating people on the country, its people and history from what I've learned living here and feeling a sense of national pride in its achievements. I am proud to be a New Zealander, holding a New Zealand passport and feeling the perceived envy of those who do not.

When I look back at my former life in San Diego, it's as if my memories are sepia-toned with nostalgia and sometimes, when there is a pang for the past, I quickly accept that the reality of living back in the States now would be very different to what I am experiencing here in New Zealand. We are indeed lucky to live in a time when old friends and family are just a phone call or an e-mail away. And there are several flights a day that leave for the USA and beyond.

As it is often said here: *"We don't know how lucky we are, mate!"*

And how lucky am I to call this place my home?

VERY.

I'm on top of the world living the life Paul and I have created with family and friends on the bottom of the world, and pervading the air is this undisturbed sense of well-being.

* * * * *

Please visit my author website at **susanctunney.com** for weekly musings, updates, quizzes and pertinent interviews about New Zealand.

Printed in Great Britain
by Amazon